Tennis

Other titles in the Science Behind Sports series:

Tennis

CARLA MOONEY

Severna Park
Middle School
Media Center

LUCENT BOOKS
A part of Gale, Cengage Learning

GALE
CENGAGE Learning·

Detroit • New York • San Francisco • New Haven, Conn • Waterville, Maine • London

LIBRARY OF CONGRESS CATALOGING-IN-PUBLICATION DATA

Mooney, Carla, 1970-
   Tennis / by Carla Mooney.
     p. cm. -- (Science behind sports)
   Includes bibliographical references and index.
   ISBN 978-1-4205-0928-1 (hardback)
1. Tennis--Juvenile literature. I. Title.
   GV996.5.M66 2013
   796.342--dc23

2012049997

Lucent Books
27500 Drake Rd
Farmington Hills MI 48331

ISBN-13: 978-1-4205-0928-1
ISBN-10: 1-4205-0928-4

Printed in the United States of America

1 2 3 4 5 6 7 17 16 15 14 13

TABLE OF CONTENTS

FOREWORD

On March 21, 1970, Slovenian ski jumper Vinko Bogataj took a terrible fall while competing at the Ski-flying World Championships in Oberstdorf, West Germany. Bogataj's pinwheeling crash was caught on tape by an ABC *Wide World of Sports* film crew and eventually became synonymous with "the agony of defeat" in competitive sporting. While many viewers were transfixed by the severity of Bogataj's accident, most were not aware of the biomechanical and environmental elements behind the skier's fall—heavy snow and wind conditions that made the ramp too fast and Bogataj's inability to maintain his center of gravity and slow himself down. Bogataj's accident illustrates that, no matter how mentally and physically prepared an athlete may be, scientific principles—such as momentum, gravity, friction, and aerodynamics—always have an impact on performance.

Lucent Book's Science Behind Sports series explores these and many more scientific principles behind some of the most popular team and individual sports, including baseball, hockey, gymnastics, wrestling, swimming, and skiing. Each volume in the series focuses on one sport or group of related sports. The volumes open with a brief look at the featured sport's origins, history and changes, then move on to cover the biomechanics and physiology of playing, related health and medical concerns, and the causes and treatment of sports-related injuries.

In addition to learning about the arc behind a curve ball, the impact of centripetal force on a figure skater, or how water buoyancy helps swimmers, Science Behind Sports readers will also learn how exercise, training, warming up, and diet and nutrition directly relate to peak performance and enjoyment of the sport. Volumes may also cover why certain sports are popular, how sports function in the business world, and which hot sporting issues—sports doping and cheating, for example—are in the news.

Basic physical science concepts, such as acceleration, kinetics, torque, and velocity, are explained in an engaging and accessible manner. The full-color text is augmented by fact boxes, sidebars, photos, and detailed diagrams, charts and graphs. In addition, a subject-specific glossary, bibliography and index provide further tools for researching the sports and concepts discussed throughout Science Behind Sports.

CHAPTER 1

The History of Tennis

Since winning her first U.S. Open in 1999, American professional tennis player Serena Williams has dominated women's tennis. As of 2012, she had won a total of fourteen Grand Slam singles titles, Olympic gold medals, and many doubles championships with her sister, Venus Williams. As Williams got older and suffered a string of injuries, many people predicted that the tennis star would soon hang up her racket and retire. Williams quickly dashed the rumors. In an interview in 2012, she declared that her love of the game would keep her playing for many more years. "I have no intention of stopping. . . . I enjoy being out there on the court so much and I've been having so much fun, so it's been great,"[1] she said.

A Global Sport

People around the world are in love with the game of tennis. Played by professionals and amateurs alike, tennis is one of the world's most popular sports. Millions play the game. Millions more like to watch it, particularly professional tournaments.

African Americans Swing the Racket

In the early twentieth century, the organization known today as the United States Tennis Association (USTA) did not admit African Americans to the majority of its events. As a result, a group of black tennis enthusiasts formed the American Tennis Association (ATA) in 1916. It was the first black sports organization in the United States.

The ATA developed its own tennis circuit in which African American tennis players could compete. The organization held its first ATA National Championships at Druid Hill Park in Baltimore, Maryland, in August 1917.

In 1940 the color barrier in tennis began to crack when the first interracial match was played. Don Budge, winner of the 1938 tennis Grand Slam, met ATA champion Jimmie McDaniel in an exhibition match. The barrier cracked even more when a young woman named Althea Gibson captured the nation's attention in the 1950s. Invited to play in the 1950 U.S. Nationals, Gibson went on to win five Grand Slam singles titles and six doubles titles.

Arthur Ashe displays the victor's trophy after his win at Wimbledon in 1975.

In the 1960s African American Arthur Ashe rose to prominence in the sport. During his career, Ashe won thirty-five amateur single titles and thirty-three professional single titles, including the 1970 Australian Open and 1975 Wimbledon. He was the first black man to play in and to win many of the sport's tournaments, opening the door for black tennis athletes who followed him. In 1997 the Arthur Ashe Stadium was built in New York and named in his honor. The stadium hosts the U.S. Open.

Professional tennis was once dominated by English and American athletes, but today top tennis players come from all over the globe. Starting in the late twentieth century, tennis moved into new markets, attracted wider audiences, and encouraged young talent worldwide. The emergence of tennis stars such as Rafael Nadal from Spain, Maria Sharapova from Russia, and Li Na from China has made tennis a truly global sport. In 2011, for the first time since the beginning of player rankings in 1975, the top ten women tennis players represented ten different countries. "Having 10 different players represent the top 10 rankings shows how truly global tennis has become,"[2] says Stacey Allaster, chairwoman and chief executive officer of the Women's Tennis Association (WTA), the global organizing body for women's professional tennis. The 2011 men's rankings also reflect tennis's global trend, with players from seven different countries on the list.

The Origins of Tennis

Although tennis is played all over the world today, it is unclear exactly how and when the game began. People have played ball games for centuries, dating back as early as ancient Egyptian and Greek societies. Some historians believe that tennis has its origins in these early ball games. Others believe the game's roots are planted in fifth-century Tuscany in Italy, where villagers played games using their bare hands to strike balls in the street.

Many historians believe that European monks in the eleventh and twelfth centuries developed one of the earliest versions of tennis. Like the Tuscan villagers centuries before them, the monks used their bare hands to bat a ball back and forth, but they did it on an indoor court. The game was called *jeu de paume*, which means "game of the palm" in French. Over time, players began wearing leather gloves to play the game. Later some players used a wooden paddle to hit and serve the ball; the paddle became the first tennis racket. By 1500, players were hitting the ball with wood-framed rackets, and the game was still typically played on indoor courts.

According to historians, *jeu de paume* became popular in monasteries across Europe in the fourteenth century. The balls used in these early games were made of wood. Over time the ball evolved into cellulose or plant-based material enclosed in leather, which made it bouncier.

A Game of Kings

The popularity of *jeu de paume* quickly spread from monasteries to the royal houses of Europe. King Louis X of France, who reigned from 1314 to 1316, was known as an avid player of *jeu de paume*. He constructed one of the first modern-style indoor tennis courts in Paris. The indoor design quickly spread to royal palaces throughout Europe. Louis died in 1316 after a particularly hard game, but his death did not dampen his country's enthusiasm for *jeu de paume*.

King Francis I of France, who reigned from 1515 to 1547, was reported to be an enthusiastic *jeu de paume* player who promoted the sport and built many courts around his country. By 1600, there were as many as two thousand courts across France. Before serving, the French players would shout the word *tenez*, a form of the French verb *tenir*, which means "to hold." Some believe this word eventually evolved into the modern name of tennis.

Not to be outdone by their rivals in France, the kings of England also adopted *jeu de paume*. During the reign of King Edward III, who ruled from 1327 to 1377, a *jeu de paume* court was built at Windsor Castle. In the 1530s, King Henry VIII, who reigned from 1509 to 1547, built an indoor tennis court at Hampton Court Palace, where the ball could be hit off the wall.

With so many kings and noblemen playing, the game eventually became known as real, or royal, tennis. Royal tennis grew in popularity and was widely played in Europe during the seventeenth and eighteenth centuries.

SET POINT

In 1988 Steffi Graf became the only tennis player to win all four Slam tournaments and the Olympic gold medal in a single year. This feat is called the Golden Slam.

An illustration from 1581 depicts a French nobleman holding a racquet for playing jeu de paume, *or tennis, which was popular among European aristocracy.*

As the sport grew in popularity, the rules and equipment became more standardized. More players began to use rackets instead of their hands to hit the ball back and forth. A typical royal tennis court was a narrow indoor court where the ball could be played off the walls. The net was 5 feet high (1.5m) at each end and 3 feet high (1m) in the middle.

When the French Revolution erupted in the late 1700s, the royal houses of France and other European nations were under siege. Interest in the royal sport declined. Other racket sports, such as racquets and squash, emerged.

In the 1840s the invention of vulcanized rubber revolutionized royal tennis. Prior to this invention, tennis balls were stuffed with wool or hair and enclosed in a material such as leather. Tennis balls made of vulcanized rubber had a lot more bounce. By the 1850s, players were experimenting with the bouncy rubber balls on outdoor grass courts.

Lawn Tennis

In 1874 Walter Clopton Wingfield, a British army officer, designed and patented a game similar to modern tennis. He called the game by two names, lawn tennis and *sphairistike*, which is a Greek word for "ball games." The name lawn tennis caught on faster because it was easier for people to say and remember.

Wingfield first introduced his game at a house party in 1873. Although it was based on royal tennis, Wingfield's game was played outdoors on a grass court. It required a level stretch of lawn, two posts, a net, rackets, and a rubber ball. Originally Wingfield designed the court to be shaped like an hourglass and tapered at the net. Wingfield also wrote the book, *The Book of the Game*, which contains a short history of tennis, instructions for play, notes on how to erect a tennis court, and his rules of the game.

Lawn tennis became an immediate success and quickly spread throughout Great Britain, Ireland, and other countries. People played tennis at private homes on the lawn and at public parks. Private cricket clubs, where members played the game of cricket with balls and bats, were also quick to take up lawn tennis.

As lawn tennis spread around the world, however, there was little consistency in how it was played from club to club. Players were confused over the rules of the game. The court shape and

SET POINT

Although tennis is officially called "lawn tennis," it is rarely played on grass courts today. Most courts are made of clay, asphalt, or concrete. Some courts are even made of rubber or plastic.

An illustration depicts British men and women playing lawn tennis in 1883. The sport's popularity spread throughout Great Britain and other European countries in the late 1800s.

size varied from place to place. To reduce the confusion, several prominent English clubs, including the All England Croquet Club at Wimbledon and the Marylebone Cricket Club, got together to establish a common set of rules.

Using the new standard rules, the All England Croquet Club announced its first annual Wimbledon tournament in 1877. The English championship was played on a rectangular lawn court and used a set of rules similar to those used in the modern tennis game. At the first Wimbledon tournament, the only event was the men's singles. Twenty-two players wearing hats and ties participated, and Spencer Gore won the first Wimbledon title. Even though he won, Gore was not impressed with the sport, later saying that he preferred cricket to tennis. He wrote, "That anyone who has really played well at cricket, [real] tennis, or even rackets, will ever seriously give his attention to lawn tennis, beyond showing himself to be a promising player, is extremely doubtful; for in all probability the monotony of the game would choke him off before he had time to excel at it."[3] In 1884 the All England Croquet Club added ladies' singles and men's doubles events to its annual Wimbledon tournament.

Tennis Comes to America

Tennis arrived in the United States in 1874, and it quickly spread across the country. One of the first people to bring tennis to the United States was Mary Outerbridge. While on vacation in Bermuda during the winter of 1874, Outerbridge watched British army officers playing lawn tennis. Fascinated by the game, she arranged for the equipment needed to play it to be sent to her home in New York. Once she returned home, Outerbridge introduced lawn tennis to her family and friends. She also helped set up the first tennis court at the Staten Island Cricket & Baseball Club. For her role in intro-

Women compete in a tennis tournament in the 1870s at the Staten Island Cricket & Baseball Club, the site of the first tennis court in the United States.

ducing lawn tennis in the United States, Outerbridge became known as the "Mother of American Tennis."

The "Father of American Tennis" is James Dwight. He organized one of the country's first tournaments in 1876 and later served for many years as the president of the organization that is known today as the United States Tennis Association (USTA). A championship tennis player himself, Dwight was instrumental in establishing American tennis as a competitive sport.

As lawn tennis grew more popular in the United States, controversies about the correct way to play grew. Nonstandard equipment, rules, and scoring caused confusion and arguments among players and clubs. In May 1881 representatives of several prominent tennis clubs met in New York City to discuss the problem. They decided to form the U.S. National Lawn Tennis Association (USNLTA), a national tennis organization that would standardize the rules of the game and develop the sport. By 1882 the USNLTA had set forth rules that were very similar to those used today. Under the standard rules, scoring, net height, and court size were consistent from club to club. In 1975 the USNLTA became known as the United States Tennis Association (USTA).

In August 1881 the USNLTA sponsored the first national tennis championship in the United States. The U.S. National Singles Championship for men was held at the Newport Casino in Newport, Rhode Island, and attracted twenty-six players. Harvard University student Richard Sears won the first title. Six years later, in 1887, the first women's tennis championship, the U.S. Women's National Singles Championship, was held at the Philadelphia Cricket Club in Philadelphia, Pennsylvania and was won by Ellen Hansell. Today, these two championships are known as the U.S. Open.

In the early days of tennis, players served the ball underhand. As a lower net became standard, serves changed. The lower net allowed for harder, flatter shots that were more difficult for an opponent to return. As a result, overhand serves became common. In the United States players served using an overhand throwing motion borrowed from baseball, and American players became some of the best servers in early tennis history. "The British players in the early years were hampered by a lack of throwing balls as they grew up. Americans became the dominant servers almost immediately, mainly because of baseball,"[4] says John Faribault, a lecturer in human performance at Baylor University who has conducted many studies on the tennis serve.

A Competitive Game

At first, people played tennis as a social activity. Before long, lawn tennis evolved into a competitive game. Organizers set up tournaments for the best players. As competitive tennis's popularity grew, tournaments attracted more players and

Suzanne Lenglen of France competes in the women's tennis event at the Olympic Games in Antwerp, Belgium, in 1920. Tennis was an Olympic sport from 1896 to 1924, and it was reintroduced in 1988.

spectators. By the early 1900s, the competitive game had spread internationally. The best players traveled around the world to tournaments in other countries. In 1913 the International Lawn Tennis Federation, which would later become the International Tennis Federation (ITF), was formed as a world governing body for tennis.

In 1900 the first international men's team competition, the International Lawn Tennis Challenge was held. A member of the Harvard University tennis team, Dwight Davis, designed the tournament format and donated a trophy to be given to the winners. The event, held in Boston Massachusetts, pitted American tennis players against British players. The U.S. team won that first competition. Today the tournament, now called the Davis Cup, is the world's largest annual international tennis competition with players from more than one hundred countries participating. In 1923 Hazel Hotchkiss Wightman launched a similar competition for women called the Wightman Cup. The American team defeated players from Great Britain in the first competition. The Wightman Cup was held annually until 1989, when organizers announced that it would be suspended indefinitely due to low interest.

Today Wimbledon; the U.S. Open; the French Open, first held in 1891; and the Australian Open, first held in 1905 are known as the Slams and are considered the most prestigious tournaments in tennis for men and women. Tennis was also added as an event in the Olympic Games in 1896 but was removed after the 1924 games. After several decades in which the International Olympic Committee and the ITF disagreed about whether professional players should be allowed to compete, tennis was restored to the Olympics in 1988.

The Golden Age of Tennis

In the 1920s the popularity of tennis increased tremendously. Players from many countries took part in tournaments around the world. Some became celebrity figures, admired for their athletic skills and style. Several players from this era became some of the sport's all-time greats.

Four of these all-time great players, Henri Cochet, Jean Borotra, Jacques Brugnon, and René Lacoste of France, became known as the "Four Musketeers." Between them, they won twenty Grand Slam titles and twenty-three Grand Slam doubles titles. The Four Musketeers also won six straight Davis Cup tournaments for France from 1927 through 1932.

American Bill Tilden won eight Grand Slam tournaments between 1920 and 1925, including six consecutive U.S. championships. Tilden also won two more championships, the U.S. and French, in 1929 and 1930, before turning

The Slams of Tennis

Today's tennis tour includes four tournaments called the Slams or the Majors. These tournaments are the most important annual tennis competitions. They offer the most points toward a player's world ranking and also the highest prize money. Each tournament is played in a different country, on three different types of court.

The four tournaments are:
- The Australian Open, played in January on a hard court in Australia.
- The French Open, played in May or June on a clay court in France.
- Wimbledon, played in June or July on a grass court in England.
- The U.S. Open, played in August or September on a hard court in the United States.

Winning all four slams in the same calendar year is called a Grand Slam. If a player wins all four slams, but not in the same year, the achievement is called a career Grand Slam.

professional. He was an instrumental player on the U.S. Davis Cup team and helped the Americans remain undefeated for most of the 1920s.

Through the late 1920s, tennis national championships and major events were only open to amateur players. In 1926 the first professional tennis tour was organized with several American and French players. With the establishment of a professional tour, a string of amateur players began turning professional. As professionals, players were paid for matches and could make a living at tennis. Yet turning professional also meant giving up the opportunity to compete in major tournaments. Once a player joined the professional tour, he or she could no longer play in the Grand Slam tournaments, which were reserved for amateur players only.

The Open Era

After World War II, television brought tennis to more people. Stations broadcast tournaments featuring the top players on international airwaves, bringing exciting world-class tennis to average people in the comfort of their own home.

The trend of players turning professional also continued. Between the mid-1920s and the 1960s, many of the best tennis players from around the world dropped their amateur status and joined the professional tour. They toured with other professional players, earned money, and made a living playing tennis. Yet all of the major tournaments, including the four Grand Slams and the Davis Cup, remained closed to professionals. Fans of the sport grew increasingly frustrated that the world's best players were excluded from competing against each other in the most prestigious tournaments.

Thousands of tennis fans watch the women's singles final at the French Open at Roland Garros in Paris in 1952. The French Open as well as the other three Grand Slam events, plus the Davis Cup, were closed to professionals until 1968.

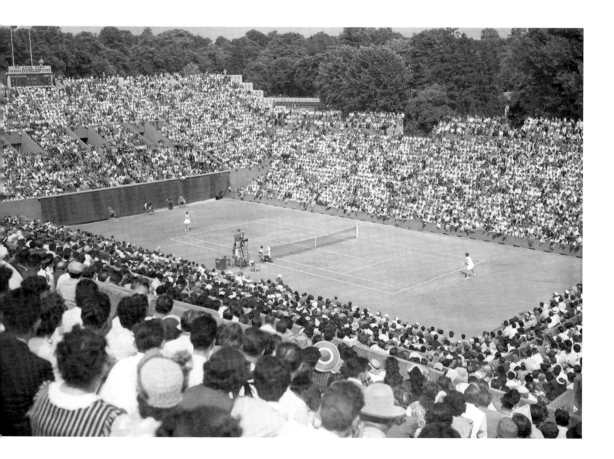

Finally in 1968 the pressure from fans and sponsors led the Lawn Tennis Association (LTA) in Britain to dissolve the difference between professional and amateur tennis players. The other major tournaments and associations soon followed the LTA's lead. As a result, tennis professionals were able to compete in all tournaments, including the four Grand Slam events. "It was momentous, it was the brave new world of tennis. People talk about all the significant moments in tennis history but to me, that was the biggest one,"[5] said Charlie Pasarell, a tennis player who would later become an influential tournament director and board member for the Association of Tennis Professionals tour.

The opening of tournaments to all players marked the beginning of the open era of tennis. All players could compete without having to choose between money and titles. Many believe that open tennis is the single biggest factor that led to today's multimillion-dollar tennis industry.

In the open era professional players formed their own associations. The Association of Tennis Professionals (ATP) formed for men in 1973, while the Women's Tennis Association (WTA) formed in 1974. Today, every major individual tournament is controlled by the ATP and WTA, except the four Grand Slam events that are controlled by the ITF.

Tennis Today

Since the open era began, significant increases in prize money, sponsorship, and television revenues have allowed the top tennis players to become some of the richest athletes in the world. For a player winning a Grand Slam tournament, the prize money is significant. For example, in the singles champions at the 2011 U.S. Open each took home a staggering $1.8 million.

According to *Forbes* magazine, Swiss player Roger Federer is the highest-paid tennis player in the world. Between July 2011 and July 2012, he earned $54.3 million. His earnings came from several sources, including tournament prize money, endorsements, exhibitions, and appearance fees.

Not as Simple as It Looks

From its early days as *jeu de paume*, tennis has evolved into a sport that requires skill, accuracy, agility, and endurance. "Tennis is an extraordinarily hard game because there is so much complexity to it. . . . If you're not ready in body and mind then it's hard to expect the best from yourself,"[6] says former Australian ATP tennis player Scott Draper.

Yet despite its complexity, tennis is popular with millions of people around the world. Like many recreational players, ESPN journalist Chris McKendry started playing tennis as a child and continues to enjoy the game as an adult. In an article for a 2012 issue of *Tennis View Magazine*, she writes, "My parents first introduced tennis to me as a child. Growing up, I played tennis during the summer, and then in fifth grade, I was introduced to USTA Junior League. . . . Tennis spoke to the athlete in me. I loved the sport. Today, I still love tennis. It sounds cliché, but it really is one sport you can play your whole life."[7]

CHAPTER 2

Training and Conditioning

Tennis places complex physical demands on a player's body. For today's game, players must possess flexibility, strength, power, agility, and speed to hit winning shots and serves. During a match, tennis players have to move quickly in all directions, change directions, and stop and start abruptly. They also need endurance to perform in matches that can last for hours.

Tennis players participate in training and conditioning programs specifically designed to improve their tennis game. If players skip part of their training program, they are less likely to perform their best. In addition, poorly conditioned athletes are more likely to injure themselves on the court.

Flexibility

Tennis players hit the ball from a variety of positions. They extend their arms to reach a wide ball or lunge forward to make a shot close to the net. To move in these and many other ways, a tennis player's muscles must be flexible. Flexibility is the quality of being easily flexed or bent. In tennis and other sports, flexibility refers to the range of movement (ROM) around a joint. If the muscles, tendons, and ligaments that hold the bones together inside a joint are too tight, they will

Tennis Injuries

Tennis injuries fall into two categories: overuse injuries and acute injuries. Overuse injuries are common and occur over time. Tennis players constantly place stress on their muscles, joints, and soft tissues through the repeated motions of tennis play. The body experiences a small tear or breakdown in its structures but does not have time to heal properly. For example, a tennis player may injure a shoulder from serving thousands of times. Players' knees endure stress from repeated pivots, twists, and violent stops and starts on the court. Overuse injuries may begin as a small ache. If not treated promptly, they can become more severe injuries. The most common overuse injuries in tennis are rotator cuff tendinitis, tennis elbow, wrist strains, back pain, and knee pain.

Knee injuries are common among tennis players.

Acute injuries occur when a sudden force or impact damages a muscle, joint, bone, or soft tissue. Instead of building up over time, acute injuries happen suddenly. Common acute injuries in tennis players are strains and torn cartilage or ligaments in the knee and muscle sprains.

restrict the joint's movement. A restricted joint will decrease a player's speed and agility. Good flexibility allows a tennis player to get to balls more quickly and efficiently. Flexibility also helps players hit balls with balance and control and can prevent injury.

Flexibility differs from person to person and among different joints in a single person. Several factors affect flexibility. A muscle's ability to stretch is a major factor in a joint's flexibility. Tight muscles limit a joint's flexibility, while loosened muscles allow a greater range of motion. Muscles stretch more when warm and supplied with an increased blood flow, which happens during warm-up exercises. Regular activity and an active lifestyle can also improve flexibility, as muscles that are not used become stiff and less flexible. Injuries to a joint or the surrounding muscles, tendons, and ligaments may temporarily decrease flexibility as pain, scar tissue, and swelling limit the joint's range of motion. After an injury, stretching exercises can usually restore a joint's full range of motion and flexibility.

Joint structure also affects flexibility and determines how far and in which direction a joint can move. For example, a wrist can move up and down, side to side, or in circles. In contrast, a knee can only move up and down. In addition, older people are usually less flexible than younger people, and men are generally less flexible than women.

Stretching

All athletes use stretching to improve flexibility. Tennis players commonly use static stretching. In static stretching a muscle is slowly and gently stretched until it feels slightly uncomfortable. Then the stretched position is held for fifteen to thirty seconds. Static stretching effectively increases the range of motion of joints and improves muscle flexibility. The International Tennis Federation (ITF) recommends that players perform a static stretching routine twice a day, preferably after exercise and in the evening.

Although static stretching can improve flexibility, it should be done after performance rather than before. Research has shown that static stretching within an hour before exercise can impair an athlete's speed, power, and strength. As a result, many coaches and players prefer another type of stretching called dynamic stretching to warm up before playing tennis. Dynamic stretching, or stretching with movement, uses constant movement of muscles to gradually increase reach, speed of movement, or both. Dynamic

SET POINT

Top tennis player Maria Sharapova trains 3 to 4 hours in the gym and 1.5 hours on the tennis court each day.

stretching is not bouncy or jerky; instead, it uses slow, controlled movements. Examples of dynamic stretches used in tennis are leg swings, arm circles, and torso twists. Dynamic stretching increases body and muscle temperature and muscle blood flow. It also readies specific joints that will be used to play tennis. Generally, tennis players perform dynamic stretches in sets of eight to twelve repetitions.

Dynamic stretching is an important part of a tennis warm-up routine, helping to prepare a player's body for the demands of tennis. It stretches muscles actively and prepares them for the forces and movements that will be experienced during tennis. Dynamic stretching also reinforces the movements that are needed to play tennis.

A tennis player holds a static stretch to improve the flexibility of his leg muscles. Static stretching is most effective when done after a workout.

Agility and Footwork

Tennis players must be able to move quickly in all directions. They must also be able to change directions frequently, stopping and starting, while at the same time maintaining balance and hitting the ball with control. In a typical tennis match, a player may make more than four directional changes during each point. They may shuffle laterally, sprint forward, and then back step quickly. If a player cannot move effectively to reach the ball in time, it does not matter how good his or her shots are.

Shahar Peer performs a drill to improve her footwork and agility during a workout as she prepares to compete in the 2012 Olympic Games.

Agility allows a tennis player to move efficiently on the court and to get into position to hit the ball accurately. Agility is defined as the ability to change the body's direction smoothly, with accuracy and using a minimal amount of muscular energy. In tennis, players use agility and footwork to return balls that may land anywhere on the court, traveling with any number of variations in spin and speed. Agility requires players to have muscular strength and power to help them decelerate (slow down) rapidly, change direction, and then accelerate (increase speed) rapidly again in a different direction.

To develop agility, many tennis players train with movement and agility drills. These drills replicate movements that the players make on the court while playing tennis. Some drills focus on lateral movement, while others focus on backward and forward movements.

Speed and Quickness

Closely related to agility, speed and quickness are vital to success in tennis. Players sprint across the court to reach a ball and return a shot. In tennis speed is the time it takes to move from one point on the court to another. Players generally run in short bursts across the court. Therefore, most speed training for tennis players focuses on acceleration and deceleration. In tennis the greatest acceleration occurs in the first eight to ten steps a player makes, while players decelerate from a run to a complete stop in only one or two strides. Exercises such as plyometrics, a method of power training that puts the muscles in a prestretch before executing a powerful contraction, develop strength and explosive power and are essential for developing a player's ability to accelerate and decelerate quickly. Sprint training can also help an athlete accelerate to top speed quickly and then stop just as fast.

Quickness in tennis is related to speed, but it is not the same as speed. Aspects of quickness in tennis include how rapidly tennis players can stop after accelerating and how well they can suddenly change direction and still keep their

Gael Monfils dashes to make a backhand return during a tournament in 2008. Elements of quickness help a tennis player react, change direction, and maintain balance when returning a shot.

balance. In tennis a split second gained by a quick first step or a quick reaction time may be the difference between successfully returning a shot or missing it.

Another aspect of quickness in tennis is being able to instantly recognize and react to a shot that an opponent has hit. This type of quickness can be thought of as response time, or the amount of time it takes for a tennis player to make the appropriate movement. Response time includes both the time needed to read the situation and choose a reaction and the time it takes for a player's muscles to contract and the body to move.

Reaction time in tennis depends heavily on anticipation. A player who can accurately predict what their opponent will do or how a shot will bounce is in a better position to play successfully than a player who does not have any idea what is going to happen next. As a result, many tennis players work on specific drills to improve their anticipation skills and reaction time. Research shows that expert tennis players frequently focus on their opponent's racket and lower arm during a match to predict their next move. Watching these areas allows a player to better anticipate the type of shot and direction of the ball.

Another key to improving reaction time is understanding the possible types of shots that an opponent can hit based on the type of court and his or her position on the court. Narrowing down the possibilities helps a player improve reaction time to a shot. The fewer choices there are, the shorter time it takes to choose a response. Knowing the tendencies of an opponent can also improve a player's reaction time. Basic scouting by watching an opponent play and studying how an opponent reacts in certain situations can give a player an advantage during a match. Finally, rehearsing footwork and movement patterns can improve a tennis player's reaction time. With practice and repetition, movement becomes faster and the response becomes automatic.

Drills for movement and reaction time improve a player's quickness. For example, a coach can hold a tennis ball out to one side or the other to indicate which way a player should move. This allows the player to hone his or her reaction to the ball and practice picking up body movement cues from an opponent.

Muscle Actions

When an athlete plays tennis, muscles throughout his or her body work together to run across the court, hit a backhand shot, or smash a serve. Each movement on the court works the body's muscles and causes them to lengthen or shorten.

Muscles move in concentric or eccentric actions. In a concentric muscle action, muscle fibers contract and shorten. When a player hits a forehand shot, the muscles in the front of the shoulder and chest shorten. The opposite action, an eccentric muscle action, occurs when the muscle fibers lengthen or stretch. During that same forehand shot,

CONCENTRIC AND ECCENTRIC MUSCLE ACTIONS

Concentric muscle actions are those in which the muscle shortens while contracting. Eccentric muscle actions are those in which the muscle elongates while contracting. In this case "contraction" refers to tensing the muscle, not shortening it. Storing and releasing elastic energy through eccentric and concentric muscle contractions powers an athlete's performance.

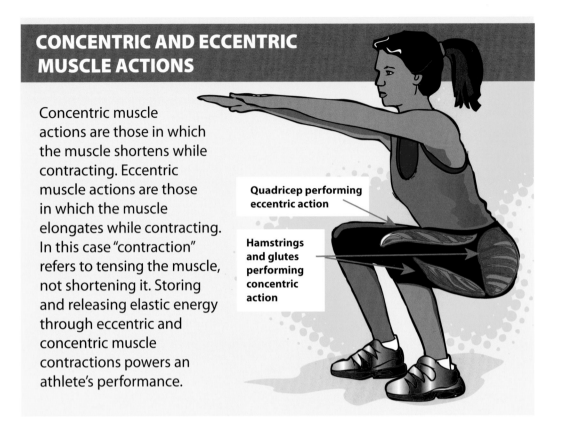

Quadricep performing eccentric action

Hamstrings and glutes performing concentric action

the muscles of the back of the shoulders and upper back lengthen in an eccentric muscle action. Eccentric muscle actions act to stabilize the body and joints and protect the body from injury.

Eccentric muscle contractions also store elastic energy, like a rubber band stores energy when stretched. When the muscle is released in a concentric contraction, the stored energy is released and allows the player to produce muscular force. To illustrate this idea, consider how high a person can jump from a standing position. If the same person squats before jumping, then the leg muscles lengthen in an eccentric contraction and store elastic energy. That energy is released during the concentric contraction of the jump, allowing the player to jump higher. Storing and releasing elastic energy through eccentric and concentric muscle contractions powers an athlete's performance.

The Muscle Behind the Movement

Muscles control all movement in the body. There are over six hundred muscles in the human body. Some function involuntary, like the heart muscle, and move without a person thinking about it. Other muscles, like the skeletal muscles, are voluntary and move in response to signals from the brain. Skeletal muscles are the muscles used when walking, talking, and playing tennis. They are attached to bones by tough bands called tendons.

A muscle works by expanding and contracting. Muscles are made of long, thin cells called fibers that are grouped together into bundles. Groups of muscle fibers work together with a nerve that makes the fibers contract or relax during movement. To move, the brain sends a signal through the nerve to the muscle group that tells a muscle to contract. When a muscle contracts, the tendon and bone move with it. Every movement of the body is caused by a muscle contraction.

Many skeletal muscles come in pairs. Muscle pairs allow the body to move an arm or leg back and forth. For example, the biceps and triceps muscles in the arm work as a pair. When the brain signals the muscles to straighten the arm, the biceps muscle relaxes, while the triceps contracts.

Muscular Strength, Power, and Endurance

Anyone watching a tennis match can see the strength, power, and endurance that today's top players bring to the game. Tennis pro Andy Roddick has been clocked hitting a serve over 150 miles per hour (241kph), while Serena Williams displays strength and power when ripping backhand shots from any position on the court. In addition, players hit shot after shot during matches that may last as long as five hours. As these players demonstrate, strength

Zheng Jie prepares to return a shot at a tournament in 2009. Tennis players rely on strength and power in their legs, core, and shoulders to cover the court quickly and hit the ball with force.

training is essential to develop the necessary speed, endurance, and power for tennis. In their book, *Complete Conditioning for Tennis,* authors Paul Roetert and Todd Ellenbecker write, "Your game will improve as you become stronger and more powerful. The speed of the ball seems to increase every year, and players need to be able to handle the power produced by their opponents and generate power themselves."[8]

Strength is the amount of force muscles can generate. In tennis muscular strength, especially in the legs, core, upper back, and shoulders, helps a tennis player's body withstand the forces of the game and play without injury. In addition, having a base level of strength in all muscles helps an athlete maintain healthy joints and keep muscles in balance. Because tennis players tend to repeat the same shots and movements, it is important that they do not develop strength imbalances between different muscles, which may lead to injury.

Related to strength, power is a player's explosiveness, or how fast his or her muscles can generate forces. Upper-body and lower-body power are important assets in tennis. Power in the legs helps a tennis player explode across the court to return a shot. Upon reaching the ball, power in the core and shoulder muscles help the player smash it over the net. A powerfully hit ball will reach an opponent more quickly, giving them less time to react and return it.

In tennis one great serve or shot is rarely enough to win a match. The top tennis players hit powerful shots and serves repeatedly, throughout an entire match. The ground stroke a player hits at the end of the match should have the same power and intensity as the strokes hit during the first few minutes of the game. Strength training for tennis often includes exercises that are performed in high repetition. This helps to build muscular endurance so players can perform their best throughout the entire match.

Strength and Power Training for Tennis

Training muscles for tennis should focus on strength, power, and endurance. To build muscle strength, athletes use resistance training, which requires the muscles to move against an opposing force. Isotonic resistance is a dynamic form of strength training that shortens and lengthens muscle fibers by exerting them against resistance, such as a constant weight or tension. For example, in a bicep curl with a 10-pound (4.5kg) weight the bicep muscle fibers shorten as the athlete moves the weight toward the shoulder. The fibers lengthen as the athlete lowers the weight. Tennis requires this type of muscle contraction in every stroke and movement.

PLYOMETRIC TRAINING

Plyometric exercises can be used to increase both upper body and lower body strength. Plyometric drills involve a rapid lengthening of a muscle, or eccentric contraction. Energy is stored in the muscle during the stretch. This is immediately followed by a shortening of the same muscle, or a concentric contraction. When the muscles are stretched rapidly, they also rebound and shorten quickly. Plyometric training teaches the muscles to develop more forceful and faster contraction speeds. The faster and more forcefully a muscle contracts, the more power an athlete has.

Tuck Jumps

Medicine Ball Slam

Lateral Obstacle Jump

Squat Throw

Exploding Pushup

With a base of muscle strength, tennis players can perform specific exercises to increase a muscle's power. Power is a combination of strength and speed. Tennis players must be able to generate explosive power for skills such as hitting the ball hard, serving an ace (a legal serve not touched by an opponent), and moving quickly around the court. The tennis players who use their strength most effectively can hit the ball the hardest and serve the fastest. These players have trained to develop power as well as strength.

Plyometrics is an effective way for tennis players to develop and improve their power. "Plyometrics improves explosive power," says Vern Gambetta, director of athletic development for the New York Mets baseball team. "This kind of training helps you get to more shots,"[9] he says. Plyometric drills involve a rapid lengthening of a muscle, or eccentric contraction. Energy is stored in the muscle during the stretch. This is immediately followed by a shortening of the same muscle, or a concentric contraction. When the muscles are stretched rapidly, they also rebound and shorten quickly. Plyometric training teaches the muscles to develop more forceful and faster contraction speeds. The faster and more forcefully a muscle contracts, the more power an athlete has.

An example of a plyometric exercise used by tennis players is squat jumps. Squatting lengthens the leg muscles, an eccentric contraction. Jumping triggers a concentric action. Performing repetitive squat jumps develops power in the leg muscles.

Aerobic and Anaerobic Fitness and Conditioning

All human activity is fueled by either an aerobic or anaerobic energy system. In an aerobic system, the body uses oxygen to convert stored energy into fuel. Aerobic activity usually lasts more than ninety seconds and uses low to moderate intensity and includes activities such as swimming and jogging. In contrast, the body uses the anaerobic system to convert stored energy into fuel without oxygen. Anaerobic activities are high intensity and shorter duration, such as sprints or pull-ups.

Playing tennis requires an athlete's body to use both aerobic and anaerobic fuel systems. In an average tennis match, a player can use three hundred to five hundred bursts of high-intensity energy when he or she sprints across the court

to cover a ground stroke or blasts a power serve. For each short, high-energy movement, a player's anaerobic energy system provides the fuel. An athlete's body creates anaerobic energy in two ways. The immediate anaerobic energy system supplies energy for six to eight seconds. It uses stored body chemicals such as adenosine triphosphate (ATP) and creatine phosphate (CP) in a chemical reaction that creates the quick burst of energy.

If the movement lasts more than ten seconds, a second anaerobic energy system kicks into gear, the short-term anaerobic energy system. It produces intense energy for a longer period, up to about ninety seconds. This anaerobic energy is released through a series of chemical reactions within the athlete's muscles. This process fuels the energy needed for each point in a tennis match. One by-product of anaerobic energy production is lactic acid. When lactic acid builds up in the muscle, the athlete feels a burning sensation.

An entire tennis match, which includes a series of high-intensity moments, can last for hours, testing an athlete's endurance. For long-term fuel, the body's aerobic energy system kicks in and allows tennis players to produce energy for a longer period. The aerobic energy system provides baseline energy over the length of a tennis match or practice session. The aerobic energy system takes in oxygen through the lungs and carries it via the bloodstream to the working tissues in the body. It uses the oxygen as a catalyst for a chemical reaction in the muscles that produces ATP or energy. In any sport, aerobic energy provides a baseline of energy and fitness. Good aerobic fitness allows a tennis player to recover more quickly between bursts of high-intensity movement. Athletes with good aerobic fitness can also clear accumulated lactic acid from their muscles more rapidly.

To perform well on the court, tennis players need to have high levels of aerobic and anaerobic fitness. Both factors are important when building a conditioning program for tennis athletes. To improve anaerobic fitness, tennis players use drills and activities that feature a relatively short period of high-intensity work followed by a period of recovery. General anaerobic drills include interval training and on-court movement drills, such as wind sprints, line drills, and side shuffles. Aerobic training activities usually involve major muscle groups, such as the legs, and are repetitive. Examples include running, swimming, stair climbing, and biking.

Starting in the late twentieth century, athletes who play tennis have become bigger, faster, and stronger. Training and conditioning to improve an athlete's strength, power, speed, and agility are critical components in performing at the highest level.

CHAPTER 3

Racket Power and Control

The world's top tennis players make hitting a ball look like a simple swing of the racket, yet using a tennis racket to hit a ball is a complex process. The player wants to swing the racket as fast as possible to generate the maximum amount of force when the racket strikes the ball. At the same time, tennis players must control the racket, not allowing the force of the ball on impact to push it backward, twist it, or bend it out of shape.

Although a racket may look simple, how it is made affects how the ball reacts to each shot the player makes. The weight, size, strings, length, and materials all affect how the racket performs. According to Rod Cross and Crawford Lindsey, authors of the book, *Technical Tennis: Racquets, Strings, Ball, Courts, Spin, and Bounce*, "matching the correct racquet to the player will always be an art, but one that is more and more based in science."[10]

The Perfect Racket

The two most important features of a racket are its power and control. A tennis player must be able to hit strokes and serves with power, sending balls that move so fast opponents have difficulty returning them. At the same time, a player must be able to hit shots with control, placing them just out of the opponent's reach in the court.

The power and control of a racket are affected by many variables, from the weight of the frame to the tension in the strings. Each factor plays a role in determining how a racket hits and how the ball responds to a shot. Determining the perfect combination of these factors is a balancing act, one that is different for each player. For example, increasing string tension decreases power but will increase control. For a powerful player, this may be a good choice. For a weaker player, a racket with more power may be more effective. Therefore, choosing the perfect racket is a uniquely personal decision.

Racket Power

A tennis racket's power is frequently described as either the ball speed off the racket or the ability of a racket to make a ball go fast. A racket with power can enable a player to hit the ball back to an opponent as fast as possible, making it harder for the opponent to return the shot. The speed of a ball coming off a racket, and therefore a racket's power, depends on two main factors, the rebound speed and the racket speed. Rebound speed is how fast the ball bounces off the racket's strings. Racket speed is how fast the player swings the racket. Together, the rebound speed plus racket speed equals the exit speed, or the speed at which the ball comes off the strings.

Rebound speed can be determined by simply dropping a ball from a specific height onto a stationary, handheld racket. The ball will rebound, or bounce, to a certain height. The ratio of the rebound height to the drop height is the fraction of energy return. If a ball is dropped from a height of 20 inches (51cm) and it rebounds 3.2 inches (8cm), then about 16 percent of the ball's energy is returned on the rebound. The square root of this number, 0.4, is the ratio of exit speed to the incoming speed of the ball. The higher the ratio, the

Evolution of the Racket

The earliest tennis rackets were made in the late 1800s. The frame was generally constructed of ash wood, because it is strong and resilient. By the 1870s, the racket head grew in size, but was small compared to today's standard. For the next one hundred years, wooden rackets remained popular. Over the years the strength and durability of wooden rackets improved as racket makers began to use thin layers of several types of wood glued together, but wooden rackets remained heavy and had small heads.

Metal rackets existed as early as 1889 but were not widely used. In 1967 Wilson Sporting Goods introduced the first popular metal racket. The steel frame was stronger and lighter than wood. In 1976 the first oversize racket head gained popularity. Its aluminum frame had a string area more than

Tennis racquets made of wood were used for around hundred years, until metal racquets were introduced in the late 1960s.

50 percent larger than the standard 65-square-inch (419sq.-cm) wooden racket. The lighter weight and larger head made tennis easier for recreational players. For professionals, the metal frames were too unpredictable. A hard, off-center shot would bend the frame and change the direction of the ball.

By 1990, graphite frames had exploded into the tennis world. Graphite frames are made from a mixture of carbon fibers and a plastic resin. They are stiffer and provide better control for advanced players. Today, graphite frames remain the most common choice for players looking for a stiff racket.

more rebound speed the racket has and the faster the ball will come off the strings.

Rebound speed is actually a measure of how much energy is lost when the ball collides with the racket. When two objects collide, each exerts a force on the other. Energy is usually transferred from one object to the other. When the ball hits the racket, the energy comes from the mass and the motion of the ball and racket. As the energy is transferred, some of it is lost. Higher rebound speeds mean that less energy is lost.

Rebound speed or power is not determined by a single property of a tennis racket. Instead, it is the combination of all of the frame's physical characteristics. A racket's weight, balance, swing weight, stiffness, head size, pattern, string, and tension all impact a racket's rebound speed and power.

Racket Control

In tennis control means being able to hit the ball to a desired location at a desired speed. A tennis player uses speed, spin, and angle to get the ball to where he or she wants it, when he or she wants it. A large portion of control depends on the player. How hard the player swings, the technique he or she uses, and how the player grips the racket can impact control.

A tennis player swings her racquet to send the ball across the court. The speed of a player's swing plus the speed at which the ball rebounds off the strings affects the ball's exit speed.

The properties of the tennis racket also affect control. When the ball hits the racket, the force of the impact causes the racket to bend and rotate backward. The harder the ball hits the racket, the more bending, rotating, and twisting will happen. The more the racket bends and rotates, the less control a player will have over which direction the ball will rebound.

The same racket properties that affect power, such as weight, weight distribution, and frame stiffness, also affect control. For example, a frame that is stiffer will be less likely to bend and twist when the ball hits it. A heavier racket is less likely to rotate upon impact.

The weight of a tennis racquet affects the speed and power of a player's swing as well as the reaction of the racquet when the ball hits it.

Racket Weight

Weight and weight distribution are two of the most important characteristics of a racket because of their impact on performance. They have a strong influence on the flow of

energy when the racket and tennis ball collide. A racket's weight and how it is distributed through the racket determine how fast a player can swing it. These factors also affect how the racket will be pushed backward, rotate, and twist when the ball hits it.

Most modern tennis rackets weigh between 8 and 12 ounces (227gr and 340gr). Recreational players tend to prefer these lighter rackets, because they are easier to swing and carry. Top tennis players, however, are stronger and more fit than recreational players. They are better able to handle heavier rackets and swing them faster. They prefer heavier rackets because they swing with more power.

Rebound speed and power depend mainly on the weight of the racket. A moving object like a racket has kinetic energy, which is the energy the object has due to motion. The kinetic energy of an object depends on the mass of the object and how fast it is moving. The more mass the object has, the more energy it has. Therefore, heavier rackets have more energy than lighter rackets.

As noted, when two objects collide, each object exerts a force on the other. Energy is usually transferred from one object to another during the collision. When a heavy racket collides with the ball, it transfers more energy to the ball than a lighter racket. Because they can transfer more energy to the ball, heavier rackets generate higher rebound speeds. If a player swings a light and a heavy racket at the same speed, the ball will leave the heavy racket faster after impact. The heavy racket has more momentum and more energy that it transfers to the ball. A player looking for raw power would choose a heavy racket.

Yet heavy rackets can be difficult to swing, especially repeatedly during the course of a three-hour tennis match or practice. Light rackets are easier to swing and can be swung faster from point A to point B. Because the ball's exit speed also involves racket speed, a lighter racket that is swung faster than a heavier racket may result in the ball leaving the strings with the same exit speed.

How the racket's weight is distributed is also a factor in its power. Rackets that are head heavy have higher rebound speeds than rackets that are handle heavy.

Balance Point

Two rackets with the same weight may feel and perform differently if their mass is distributed differently. The balance point of a racket is the point along its length where the racket will balance on a thin support, like the edge of a ruler. A racket that balances halfway along its length from the butt to the top of the head is evenly balanced. If the balance point is more than halfway up the racket, it is head heavy. If the balance point is less than half the racket length, the racket is head light.

The difference between a head-heavy and head-light racket can be felt easily by holding one of each horizontally in the hand. Although the two rackets may have the same mass, the head-heavy one will feel heavier in the hand. This is because the weight of a head-heavy racket is farther away from the hand, and the player has to use a firmer wrist to keep the racket horizontal. Head-light rackets are easier to swing and are used for hitting volleys and net play. Head-heavy rackets also hit with more power. Balanced rackets provide a little bit of both power and ease of play.

Swing Weight

Even if two tennis rackets have the same weight and balance point, they may have different swing weights. Swing weight is not a measure of a racket's total weight but instead is a measure of the distribution of its weight. Swing weight describes how heavy a racket feels when it is swung through the air. Head-heavy rackets have higher swing weights than head-light rackets. With added weight to its handle, a racket's total weight will increase, but its swing weight will decrease.

When a player swings a racket, it moves in a circular motion around a center, usually around the butt end of the racket handle. Higher swing weight rackets resist the circular movement more, which makes them feel heavier when being swung. The racket will accelerate less and rotate less quickly around the circle's center. A racket with a lower swing weight, however, will accelerate more quickly around the circle's center and feel lighter to the player even if the racket has a higher total weight.

At the same time, impact with the ball applies a force to the racket. When a ball hits a racket with a higher swing weight, it is less likely to change the racket's motion. The racket head has more power and deflects less on impact, which makes the racket more stable. For rackets with lower swing weights, the ball's impact will more easily change the racket's motion. It will be more likely to twist or rotate. This movement decreases a player's control because it can change the direction of the ball off the strings.

Each player must decide whether to choose a racket with a high swing weight or a low swing weight. Rackets with higher swing weights may have a lower final swing speed but less shock and more control when the ball pushes against the racket. Lower swing weights allow a player to achieve greater racket acceleration and swing speed but may cause greater shock and less control on impact.

Swing weight also affects power. If the racket has a higher swing weight, then more of the power comes from the racket itself and the player does not need to swing as fast. With a lower swing weight, a player must increase the swing speed to generate more power.

Racket Stiffness and Vibrations

The collision between the ball and the racket's strings can cause a racket to bend and vibrate. A racket vibrates the most around its edges. The amount of vibration at collision depends on how hard the ball is hit, how flexible the racket frame is, and where the ball hits the strings.

Racket stiffness increases as frame thickness increases. A stiff frame will bend less than a flexible frame when it collides with the ball. As the ball rebounds from the strings, a flexible frame may wiggle back and forth and vibrate rapidly through a large area. The high level of vibration in a flexible racket causes the jarring sensation that a player feels in the arm after a hard shot. Both ends of the racket vibrate and the player's hand and forearm shake back and forth.

Where the ball impacts the strings also affects a racket's vibrations. When the ball hits the middle of a racket's strings, there are little to no frame vibrations. If a player hits the ball away from the middle of the strings, then the impact causes more frame vibrations.

Sweet Spots

When a player hits a shot that feels good, he or she is said to have hit the racket's sweet spot. Although tennis players have talked about a racket's sweet spot for decades, it was not officially defined until 1981 in a technical paper published in the *American Journal of Physics*. In fact, there is more than one sweet spot in a tennis racket. In the middle

THE TENNIS RACKET—Sweet Spot and Dead Spot

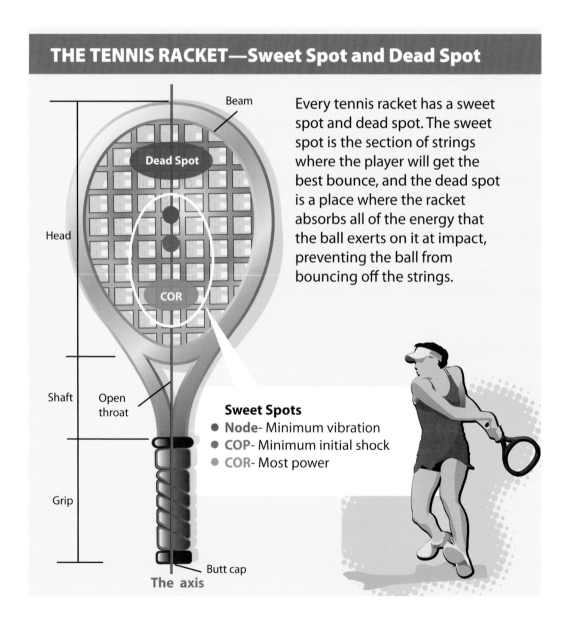

Every tennis racket has a sweet spot and dead spot. The sweet spot is the section of strings where the player will get the best bounce, and the dead spot is a place where the racket absorbs all of the energy that the ball exerts on it at impact, preventing the ball from bouncing off the strings.

Beam

Dead Spot

Head

COR

Shaft

Open throat

Grip

Butt cap

The axis

Sweet Spots
- **Node**- Minimum vibration
- **COP**- Minimum initial shock
- **COR**- Most power

A Racket's Dead Spot

A tennis racket's dead spot is an area located near the top of the racket. When a ball hits the dead spot, it does not bounce off the strings. Instead, the racket absorbs all of the energy that the ball exerts on it at impact. The player feels a maximum shock in the hand from the impact of the ball. This happens because the effective mass of the racket at that point is equal to the mass of the ball. If a ball of a certain mass hits head-on with another object of the same mass at rest, then the moving ball stops dead and transfers all of its energy to the object.

of the strings, one sweet spot, called the vibration node, is a spot where there is little to no frame vibration when the ball hits the strings. The vibration node line is a curved line that extends from the middle of the strings to points at about the ten o'clock and two o'clock positions on the racket face. An impact with the ball anywhere along the node line will not cause vibrations in the racket frame or handle, although the strings themselves will vibrate. If the ball hits near the ten o'clock or two o'clock points, though, then the racket may twist in the player's hand. Imagine a straight line down the racket's center axis from the tip to the handle; the place where this line intersects the node line is the node sweet spot. If a player hits the ball exactly at this spot, there will be no frame vibrations and no racket twist.

Another sweet spot is called the center of percussion (COP). It is located a few inches closer to the throat of the racket than the vibration node sweet spot. When the ball hits the racket, the racket exerts a force on the ball. The ball exerts an equal and opposite force on the racket. The impact of these forces can be seen by the rebound of the ball off the strings and felt by the racket handle pushing back against the player's hand. As a result of this handle push, the player's hand rotates backward around an axis through the wrist and a shock travels through the player's arm. When the ball hits on the COP, however, the two forces are equal and opposite and there is no net force on the hand or forearm. As a result, the player feels no jarring of the hand or arm.

Importance of the Strings

A tennis racket's strings are an important factor in its performance. Strings enable the ball to leave the racket with high speed without the player having to swing the racket very fast. This is why tennis players use rackets with strings instead of simple wooden paddles. The strings form a woven pattern inside the head of the racket. There are several materials that are used to make strings, including natural gut, nylon, polyester, and Kevlar. The type of string used in a racket and how it is strung can have a significant impact on a player's performance.

String tension varies from player to player. The string tension of a racket is the pressure under which the strings are secured to the frame. The tighter the strings are, the higher the string tension. Most players prefer string tension between 50 and 70 pounds (23kg and 32kg). The amount of tension affects the racket's power and control.

Tennis balls do not store and return energy efficiently. As previously noted, when two objects collide, each exerts a force on the other and energy is usually transferred from one to the other. Some energy may be lost during this process. When hit, the tennis ball loses about 45 percent of the energy applied to it. For example, if a ball is dropped from a height of 100 inches (254cm) onto a hard surface, then the ball will rebound only about 55 inches (140cm), losing 45 percent of its initial energy. In contrast, when a tennis ball hits a racket, the strings stretch and absorb the energy, and they return about 90 percent of that force when the ball rebounds. If the strings are more flexible and have a lower tension, then they will stretch more and store more energy. The ball will have more energy and speed when it rebounds off the strings. In the same manner, higher tension strings are harder and will cause the ball to deform on impact and lose energy, causing it to rebound slower off the strings.

Both the tennis ball and the strings of a racquet are deformed upon impact. The energy and speed at which the ball bounces off the racquet is dependent upon the tension of the strings.

How much the strings stretch upon collision with the ball also influences a racket's control. More flexible, stretchy strings strung at a lower tension allow a ball to stay longer on the strings at impact. The time that the ball stays on the strings is called the dwell time. The longer the dwell time, the greater impact a slight change in the racket's angle from a wrist flex or motion will have on the ball's direction. This can lead to a loss of control if the racket changes its angle while the ball is moving with the racket. In addition, balls hit off looser strings tend to have a higher trajectory, because they stay on the strings for a longer period as the racket tilts upward and rises during the swing.

String Type and Pattern

The type of string can also affect a racket's power and control. Strings can be made of many materials, including natural gut (from a part of a cow's intestines) and synthetic (man-made) products, such as nylon and polyester. The different materials impact string stiffness. Natural gut strings tend to be more elastic, while synthetic strings tend to be stiffer.

How a string plays depends on its stiffness. String stiffness is measured by how much it stretches when hit by the ball. The more the string stretches, the softer it is. The less the string stretches, the stiffer it is. Higher stiffness leads to more control, less power, and less comfort for the player. Stiffer strings experience a shorter dwell time and less string deflection. Less time on the strings means less time

A racquet's strings can be made of materials of varying stiffness, which in turn affects a player's control and power.

for the racket to twist and alter the ball's direction, which improves control. The higher impact force and less string deflection causes the ball to deform more upon impact and lose energy resulting in less power. Softer strings give more power because the strings bend to cup the ball upon impact, causing less ball deformation and energy loss. Longer time on the strings leads to less control.

Most modern professional players use a polyester string, which is stiffer and thicker than conventional gut and nylon strings. The stiff polyester strings enable top players to hit balls with more control. "People often talk about how racket technology has changed tennis, but I would argue the string technology has had a greater impact,"[11] says former U.S. Open finalist Todd Martin.

The spacing of the stringing pattern, or how far apart the strings are on the racket, can also affect how a racket plays. A denser pattern with more strings per inch will play stiffer, as if it had a higher string tension. If the strings are farther apart, then the racket will play as if the tension were lower. Open patterns generally increase string movement, which is caused by the ball pushing the main strings to the side.

Although two tennis rackets may look identical, they may in fact play very differently. Knowing the science behind a racket allows players to make the best choice for their game.

CHAPTER 4

The Science of the Bounce

In a split second, a tennis ball soars over the net and bounces off the court surface. Then it collides with a racket's strings, rebounds, and bounces off the court again. After years of watching tennis balls bounce off courts, the world's top tennis players have learned how to anticipate exactly how the ball will bounce, how fast it will travel, and where it will land. Almost instinctively, they seem to know when to move forward or backward.

How the ball bounces, its height, the speed at which it comes off the court, the angle it takes, and how it spins depend on the properties of the ball and the court. For every court and player type, there are a variety of balls. Harder, fast-speed balls can be used on slower court surfaces, while larger, slow-speed balls are designed for faster court surfaces. There is even a special type of ball for use in high altitude locations. All balls must play consistently and be durable enough to withstand repeated high-speed impact with the court.

Evolution of the Ball

Centuries ago, tennis balls in France were made of wool or cloth and encased in leather. By 1870, players batted hollow rubber tennis balls across the net. A few years later, rubber

Testing Tournament Balls

At professional tennis tournaments, the tennis balls are tested regularly to make sure they meet the required weight, diameter, and bounce. The requirements are:

- Weight between 1.975 and .095 ounces (56gr and 59.4gr).
- Diameter between 2.57 and 2.87 inches (6.54cm and 7.30cm).
- Bounce to a height between 53 and 58 inches (135cm and 147cm) when dropped from a height of 100 inches (254cm) onto a concrete slab.

tennis balls were covered in a white flannel cloth. Covering the rubber ball in cloth made it play better, allowing the racket to grip it for spin. It also made the ball more durable. Eventually, the hollow rubber ball was filled with air to pressurize it and improve its bounce. A fuzzy melton cloth replaced the original stitched flannel cloth.

Historically, tennis balls were either black or white. In 1972 the International Tennis Federation (ITF) introduced yellow tennis balls into the rules of tennis. The yellow color made the balls easier to see on television.

Today, modern tennis balls used in competition meet ITF and United States Tennis Association (USTA) specifications. The ball's size, weight, rebound, and compression follow certain standards, ensuring that the balls used in competition are similar and no player has an advantage over another player. Recreational players may use any type of ball, but in order to follow the rules of tennis the balls must be ITF or USTA approved.

Properties of the Ball

Most tennis balls are filled with pressurized air. The air presses against the inner walls of the ball's hollow rubber core, which makes the rubber walls stiffer, like the air pumped into a balloon makes it stiffer. When the ball hits a racket or the court, the pressure makes it bounce.

The rubber of most balls is slightly permeable to air, which means the air inside slowly leaks out of the ball over time. Air molecules move from high-pressure areas (inside the ball) to lower-pressure areas (outside the ball). To keep the air from leaking before the ball is sold, tennis ball makers package the balls in special pressurized cans. This keeps the ball

A player pulls a metal tab to release the seal on a pressurized can of tennis balls. Pressurization helps keep the air molecules inside the tennis balls and maintains their ability to bounce.

pressure steady until the can is opened. Then the balls are exposed to normal atmospheric pressure, and the internal air begins to seep out through the rubber walls. As this happens, the ball loses its bounce and is said to be "dead." Tennis balls can lose their bounce quickly. At Association of Tennis Professionals (ATP) and Women's Tennis Association (WTA) tournaments, officials change the ball several times during a match.

Keeping a ball at a steady temperature will improve its performance. Warm balls bounce higher than cold balls, because the warm temperature causes the gas inside the ball to expand, increasing the pressure on the ball's inner walls. At Wimbledon, the balls are stored in a special refrigerated container, which keeps them at a constant 68°F (20°C).

Some tennis balls have an internal air pressure that is the same as the outside air pressure. These pressureless balls last longer than less-expensive pressurized balls because the air cannot leak out and leave the ball dead. Pressureless balls have thicker rubber walls that generate the ball's bounce, but they have a different feel and are not as bouncy as a brand-new pressurized ball.

Modern tennis balls are covered with fuzzy cloth, made from a thick, tightly woven wool. The fuzzy fabric generates friction when the ball hits a tennis racket or the court. Friction is the force created when two surfaces move against each other. Without friction, the ball would slide away when it hit the racket or the court. The fuzzy fabric helps the ball to grab onto surfaces and then bounce away.

Bounce of the Ball

Although a tennis ball only hits the court for a brief second, the bounce it takes after impact has an enormous impact on a tennis match. During the split-second bounce, a ball changes speed, direction, and rate of spin. Alter the bounce slightly and all of these will change as well. How the ball bounces affects the strokes and strategy a player chooses during a match.

A bouncing tennis ball illustrates Newton's third law of motion. When the ball hits the court, the ground force pushes the ball vertically, which causes the ball to bounce.

When a ball bounces off the court, two forces affect how it moves. A vertical force, called a ground-reaction force, pushes up on the ball and causes it to rise or bounce. At the same time, a friction force pushes horizontally against the ball, slowing it down and causing it to spin. According to Newton's third law of motion, one of three ideas about motion developed by physicist and astronomer Isaac Newton in the eighteenth century, when a force or action acts upon a body, there is an equal and opposite reaction force. In tennis the force from the ball hitting the court is the action, while the ground force of the court pushing vertically on the ball is the reaction. The ground-reaction force causes the ball to bounce.

The magnitude of the ground-reaction force pushing up on the ball depends on the speed of the ball and the hardness of the court and ball. When the court is soft, the ball's impact deforms the court surface. If the surface is soft and does not bounce back quickly enough, some of the ball's energy

Newton's Laws of Motion

Isaac Newton (1642–1727) was an English physicist and mathematician who developed three basic ideas about motion. Scientists call his ideas Newton's laws of motion.

The first law of motion says that an object at rest tends to stay at rest, and an object in motion tends to stay in motion at the same speed and in the same direction, unless acted upon by an unbalanced force. A ball will not move unless it is pushed on one side in an unbalanced force. Similarly, a ball will not stop moving unless something pushes against it in the opposite direction.

The second law of motion says that the greater the mass of an object, the greater the force needed to move the object. If a tennis player swings two rackets of different masses, he or she will have to use more force to move the heavier racket at the same speed. This law can be expressed in this equation: Force = mass (weight) X acceleration (speed), or $F = ma$. Using this formula, if the weight and speed of an object is known, then the force being applied to it can be calculated.

The third law of motion says that for every action, there is an opposite and equal reaction. Forces are found in pairs. When a person sits in a chair, his or her body exerts a force downward on the chair. The chair exerts an equal force upward. If it did not, the chair would collapse.

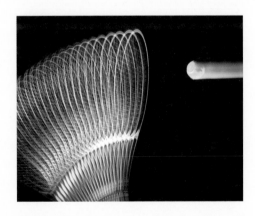

The pending impact of a racquet and a ball demonstrates Newton's first law of motion.

is lost and cannot be used to help the ball bounce high. In this case, the ground-reaction force pushing on the ball is weaker. Alternately, hard courts deform less when the ball hits. This leaves more energy for the upward force to push the ball higher and faster in its bounce.

The faster a ball's vertical speed after the bounce, the higher it will bounce. Clay courts are some of the hardest surfaces. A ball's vertical bounce will be higher and faster on clay as compared to a slower and lower bounce on a softer grass court.

Friction Forces

The second force that impacts a ball's bounce is called friction. Friction is created when two surfaces move against each other. Friction occurs every day. It allows a person to walk and run without sliding. It helps a tennis player swing a racket without it slipping out of his or her hand. In tennis friction pushes horizontally against the ball, slowing it down and causing it to spin.

Sliding friction occurs when one surface slides on another surface, such as when the ball hits and slides on the court. Sliding friction acts in the opposite direction of the ball's movement and slows the sliding motion. Sliding friction slows a ball when it hits the court. It also slows a player who slides as he or she runs on a slippery court surface.

Rolling friction occurs when the ball rolls on the court. Compared to sliding friction, rolling friction is a much weaker force. A ball rolled across the court will travel without slowing much. In comparison, a ball that slides across the court will slow much faster because of the stronger action of sliding friction on it.

Friction plays a significant role in how a ball bounces. When a ball hits the court surface, it typically does so at an angle. It starts to squash and slides along the surface. Friction pushes on the ball in the opposite direction of its slide, parallel to the surface. Friction force slows the bottom of the ball but does not act on the top of the ball. As a result, the top of the ball moves forward at a faster rate than the bottom of the ball. This causes the ball to rotate and spin. That is why most balls rotate with topspin after bouncing. If the ball was spinning before impact, then friction force may change the way it is spinning.

On a rough surface, friction can cause the ball to come to a complete stop for a split second. When the bottom of the ball comes to a stop, it is said to be biting the surface. If the court surface is slippery, then the ball will slide longer, and it will take longer for it to come to a complete stop. The bottom of the ball stops sliding, but the top keeps moving forward, which pulls the ball forward.

Rebound Angle

When a tennis ball hits the court, it bounces or rebounds at an angle. How it leaves the court depends in part on the angle at which it hits the surface. According to the laws

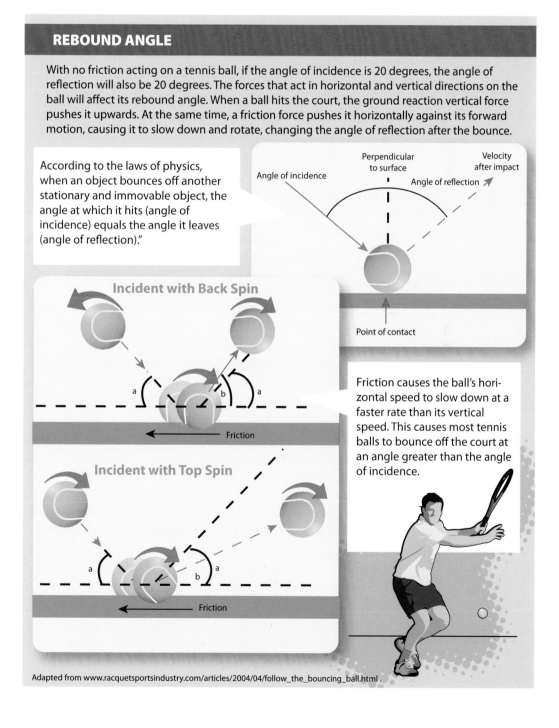

REBOUND ANGLE

With no friction acting on a tennis ball, if the angle of incidence is 20 degrees, the angle of reflection will also be 20 degrees. The forces that act in horizontal and vertical directions on the ball will affect its rebound angle. When a ball hits the court, the ground reaction vertical force pushes it upwards. At the same time, a friction force pushes it horizontally against its forward motion, causing it to slow down and rotate, changing the angle of reflection after the bounce.

According to the laws of physics, when an object bounces off another stationary and immovable object, the angle at which it hits (angle of incidence) equals the angle it leaves (angle of reflection)."

Perpendicular to surface

Velocity after impact

Angle of incidence

Angle of reflection

Point of contact

Incident with Back Spin

a

b

a

Friction

Friction causes the ball's horizontal speed to slow down at a faster rate than its vertical speed. This causes most tennis balls to bounce off the court at an angle greater than the angle of incidence.

Incident with Top Spin

a

b

a

Friction

Adapted from www.racquetsportsindustry.com/articles/2004/04/follow_the_bouncing_ball.html .

of physics, when an object bounces off another stationary and immovable object, the angle at which it hits (angle of incidence) equals the angle it leaves (angle of reflection). Therefore with no friction acting on the ball, if the angle of incidence is 20 degrees, the angle of reflection will also be 20 degrees. As a result, if the tennis ball comes in at a small angle, it will usually bounce off at a similar small angle. Balls that hit the court at a steep angle will usually bounce off at a steep angle.

The forces that act in horizontal and vertical directions on the ball also will affect its rebound angle. When a ball hits the court, the ground reaction vertical force pushes it upward. At the same time, a friction force pushes it horizontally against its forward motion, causing it to slow down and rotate. Friction causes the ball's horizontal speed to slow down at a faster rate than its vertical speed. This causes most tennis balls to bounce off the court at an angle greater than the angle of incidence.

Characteristics of the Court

Tennis courts can have many different surfaces, including clay, grass, wood, concrete, asphalt, or acrylic. Some are smooth, while others are rough. Some are soft, while others are hard, with many variations in between. Clay, concrete, asphalt, and acrylic courts are hard, while grass is one of the softest court surfaces. Grass courts are also smooth, and clay courts are rough. Each surface affects how the ball bounces on the court and its height, speed, and spin after a bounce. How the ball bounces on the surface determines if a court plays slow or fast.

A court's coefficient of restitution (COR), the ratio of the ball's vertical speed after the bounce to its speed before the bounce, measures the court's surface hardness. If the vertical speed after the bounce is faster on one court compared to another, the ball will bounce higher on the first court. For example, if a grass court has a COR of approximately 0.6 and a clay court has a COR of 0.85, a ball will vertically bounce higher and faster on the clay court.

A second characteristic, the roughness of the court surface, affects the ball's horizontal speed after it bounces. If the

ball slows down a lot after bouncing, then the court is considered slow. If the ball's horizontal speed does not change much after the bounce, then the court is fast.

In tennis the horizontal speed of the ball after the bounce depends on the amount of sliding friction generated between the ball and the court on impact. Different court surfaces present more or less friction force to the ball. Smooth court surfaces generate less friction. If the friction is low, then the ball will lose little of its horizontal speed when it bounces and the court will play fast. In contrast, rough courts have a higher level of friction with the ball. The ball will lose a larger fraction of its

Clay courts, like the ones at Roland Garros where the French Open is played, have a rough surface that cause a high level of friction on the ball, which results in slower play.

horizontal speed, making the court play slow. A court's friction is measured by the coefficient of friction (COF), which is the force required to move two sliding surfaces over each other, divided by the force holding them together. Every tennis court surface has a different COF against a tennis ball, usually between 0 and 1. The higher the COF, the more friction there will be between the court and the ball, which slows the ball's horizontal speed after it hits the court. A slippery surface may have a COF of 0.1, while a rougher surface may have a COF of 0.9. Grass courts are generally slipperier with lower COFs, while clay courts are rougher and have higher COFs. For an example of how surface roughness impacts friction, imagine pushing a heavy object across a horizontal surface. If the COF of the surface is 0.5, then it will take a horizontal force of 10 pounds (4.5kg) to slide a 20-pound (9kg) object across the surface at a constant speed. If the surface is rougher and its COF is 0.8, then it will take more force, 16 pounds (7.3kg), to slide the same object at the same constant speed.

Over time, repeated play on a rough court may wear it down and smooth it, reducing friction and making the court faster. Tennis clubs will frequently resurface these courts, sometimes covering them with a paint and sand mixture. The roughness of the sand creates high friction between the court surface and the ball, slowing it down.

Players on the court often use a ball's rebound angle to judge whether the court plays fast or slow. This is possible because friction also changes the ball's rebound angle. The more friction between the ball and the court, the larger the rebound angle will be. Higher friction will slow the ball's horizontal speed more than its vertical speed. This results in a steeper angle bounce. With less friction, the rebound angle will be smaller because the ball's horizontal speed is not slowed as much. Players know that if balls tend to bounce at higher angles, the court is probably slow and the ball will take longer to reach the player. If balls bounce off the court at lower angles, the court is probably playing fast. The player adjusts to have his or her racket ready sooner.

Playing on Different Courts

Some players prefer slow courts, while others would rather play on fast courts. Slow courts give players more time to run down shots, which may lead to longer rallies. This type of court favors players who are steady baseline players (players who prefer to play ground strokes from the backcourt instead of coming forward to the net) and make few mistakes. Players who prefer fast courts do not want the court surface to slow down their shots. This type of court favors strong hitters who win by overpowering their opponents.

When the COR is the same for both courts, the ball will rebound at a lower angle on the fast court than it will on the slow court. Players on the fast grass of Wimbledon will have less time to get to the ball than when they play on slower clay at the French Open.

Players can adapt their game and equipment to perform at their best on different courts. On a slow court, a player can swing harder or reduce the tension to his or her racket strings. These strategies will add power that is lost on a slow court. On a fast court, a player will have more difficulty controlling his or her shots. To adapt, the player can increase the tension in the strings or make the racket more head light to increase control.

CHAPTER 5

Getting the Ball in the Box

E xperienced tennis players know just how to hit a ball to send it where they want it to go. With each shot, they can usually predict where the ball will travel and the path it will take. What they may not realize is that the laws of physics determine how a tennis ball moves. With each shot, three main forces act on a ball: gravity, drag, and lift.

Aerodynamics of a Tennis Ball

When a player hits a ball into the air, Newton's laws of motion determine the ball's path. According to Newton's first law, the moving ball will stay in motion in a straight line unless an external force acts on it to change its path or stop it. In the air, several forces act on the ball. The forces of gravity, drag, and lift interact to determine the ball's path.

Gravity, the natural force of attraction exerted by a celestial body upon objects at or near its surface, pulls objects toward the center of the earth. Gravity keeps a person on the ground. Without gravity, a person or object would float like an astronaut in space. In tennis gravity pulls the ball toward the earth as it travels through the air. This makes the ball curve down and eventually hit the court instead of traveling in a straight line parallel to the ground. The force of gravity on the ball is exactly equal to the weight of the ball.

The surface of a tennis ball is fuzzy, which disrupts the flow of air around the ball and creates drag. The more a ball is used, the fuzzier it becomes, and thus drag is increased.

As the ball moves through the air, the air resists the motion of the ball. The force of this resistance is called drag. Drag pushes the ball backward and slows it down. The size of the drag force depends on several factors, including the size and speed of the ball, the surface of the ball, and air conditions. The fuzzy surface of a tennis ball disrupts the airflow around the ball in flight, creating more drag. When a tennis ball is worn, it becomes frayed and fuzzier. This increases the drag force acting on it, making the ball move slower in the air. That is why many tennis players prefer to use newer balls with less fuzz.

A third force called lift also acts on the ball in flight. Lift pushes the ball perpendicular to the ground. When an airplane flies, its wings generate lift, which pushes the plane up and allows it to fly. A spinning tennis ball also generates lift. Like drag, the size of the lift force depends on several factors, including the air conditions and the speed of the ball. If a tennis ball spins, then the speed of its rotation also affects lift.

Putting a Spin on the Ball

Today's top tennis professionals know that the key to each shot is the spin they put on the ball. In addition to the forces of gravity, drag, and lift, the direction and speed of a ball's spin affect how it travels through the air. A tennis ball with spin will change its trajectory through the air. Unlike a ball with no spin, the spinning tennis ball will dive, float, or curve. The higher the rate of spin, the more impact it will have on the ball's motion. Spin also affects how a ball bounces off the court and the angle it takes after the bounce.

Good players use spin to control where they hit the ball, just as they use ball speed and bounce angle to hit shots that are difficult for opponents to return. Players create spin by adjusting the speed, angle, and tilt of their racket when they hit the ball. There are three main types of spin used in tennis: topspin, backspin, and sidespin.

Topspin rotates the ball in the same direction that the ball is traveling. Topspin combines with gravity's downward pull on the ball. It causes the ball to curve down onto the court more quickly than a ball hit without spin. Tennis players like to hit balls with topspin, because it makes it easier for them to hit the ball hard and still get it in the baseline (the boundary line at either end of a tennis court). A ball hit with topspin will hit the court at a steeper angle, causing it to bounce higher. The spin also causes the ball to accelerate

when it hits the court and shoot forward, giving an opponent less time to react to the shot.

Balls can also be hit with backspin or sidespin. Backspin rotates the ball in the opposite direction it is traveling. A ball hit with backspin will fight against gravity. Backspin will tend to make a ball stay up or float longer than a ball hit without spin. Backspin also causes the ball to slow down. Sometimes, it may even jump backward when it hits the court. Sidespin occurs when a ball spins to the right or left around a vertical axis. Balls hit with sidespin will curve or slice to the right or left as they move through the air.

To hit a shot with spin, players move their rackets across the back of the ball as they hit it. As the racket strings contact the ball, they slide across the back of the ball and grip it. The sliding and gripping motions pull the ball in the same direction that the strings are moving. This causes the ball to

Serena Williams returns a shot with her racquet angled forward in order to put topspin on the ball.

Rubber Bands and Energy

Muscles are often compared to rubber bands in how they store and release energy. Stretching a rubber band requires work. This changes the arrangement of the rubber band and increases the potential energy stored in it. When it is released, the rubber band releases the energy and restores itself to its original form. Another example is a bow and arrow. When the drawstring of a bow is pulled back, energy is stored in the string. When released, this energy makes the arrow shoot forward. The bow's drawstring returns to its original form and position. The muscles of the human body work in a similar manner. They hold elastic energy when stretched. When contracted, they release the elastic energy and return to their original form.

spin in that direction. If the racket moves upward when hitting the ball, the ball spins forward in a topspin. If the racket head moves downward, then the ball spins backwards in a backspin. Pulling the racket sideways generates a sidespin.

The Magnus Force

Why does spin make a tennis ball move in different ways? The reason was discovered in 1853 by German chemist and physicist Heinrich Gustav Magnus, who found that as a ball moves through the air, the way the air flows around it affects the ball's trajectory. If the ball is not spinning, then the air will flow around the ball with equal pressure on all sides and not change the ball's trajectory. If the ball spins as it moves through the air, then it creates a pressure difference between its two sides. This occurs because the spinning ball drags some air around with it. The side of the ball that is spinning in the opposite direction of the ball's flight moves against the flow of air around the ball. This creates more drag on that side of the ball, slowing it down, and increasing the pressure on it. At the same time, the opposite side of the ball is spinning in the same direction as the airflow around the ball, so it experiences less drag, moves faster, and has less pressure on it. The difference in pressure between the two sides causes the ball to curve in the direction of the lower pressure side. This principle is called the Magnus effect.

In tennis the Magnus effect affects the flight of a ball hit with spin. A ball hit with topspin spins forward as it travels through the air. The top of the ball moves against the flow of the air around the ball. The bottom of the ball, however, spins in the same direction as the airflow around the ball. This creates more drag on the top of the ball and less drag on the bottom of the ball. Drag makes the air move slower over the top of the ball and faster under the bottom. The slower-moving air over the top exerts more pressure on the ball than the faster moving air exerts upward on the bottom of the ball. Because of the Magnus effect, the heavier force pushing down on a ball hit with topspin causes it to curve down toward the court.

A ball hit with backspin experiences the opposite effect. The ball rotates from bottom to top as it travels through the air. The bottom of the ball travels against the flow of air, creating more drag. Airflow travels faster over the top of the ball, which travels in the same direction as the airflow. As a result, there is greater air pressure underneath the ball, which causes it to resist the downward pull of gravity for a longer period.

Ground Strokes

To win a match, a tennis player must be able to hit great ground strokes, which are either forehand or backhand swings of the racket at a ball that has bounced from the ground. Ground strokes are integral to the game of tennis. Players hit ground strokes to return their opponents' serve. Competitive tennis players need a lot of energy to hit ground strokes effectively, and they must efficiently transfer that energy from their muscles to the ball.

A boy winds up to return a shot using the kinetic chain of muscles through the length of his body in order to generate the energy and power needed to strike the ball.

A player transfers energy from his or her body to the ball through the tennis racket. The energy used in a shot can come from stored energy (elastic energy) or from kinetic energy (energy from movement). Elastic energy is stored in the player's muscles and tendons under tension. Kinetic energy is the energy the body obtains through the motion involved in the work necessary to swing the racket and make the ball move from a resting position to its desired speed.

The human body is like a chain, with different body parts linked together. For example, the foot is linked by the ankle joint to the leg, which is linked by the knee joint to the thigh, and so on. When playing tennis, the stretched muscles of the player's abdomen, forearm, chest, hip, and leg hold elastic energy. A tennis player's feet pushing on the court builds ground-reaction forces. These forces are transferred sequentially through the legs, hips, trunk, shoulder, arm, and racket. Elastic energy moves from one body segment to the next. Each movement in the chain builds upon the previous motion, combining to generate the racket speed. This linked chain, called the kinetic chain, provides the force behind a player's swing. If any part of the chain is not strong or flexible enough, then the elastic energy will not transfer efficiently through the chain. This will result in less power when the racket strikes the ball.

The transfer of energy through the kinetic chain involves the stretch-shortening cycle of the muscles involved in the hitting the shot. The stretch-shortening cycle starts with the active stretching of the muscle, followed immediately by a forceful shortening of the muscle. For example, during a forehand shot, the chest and shoulder muscles are stretched or loaded as the torso rotates into the shot. The active stretch of these muscles stores elastic energy in them and the surrounding tendons. The energy is released as the muscle snaps or rebounds. If the player times the swing correctly, this energy is transferred through the racket to the ball, sending it back over the net with power and speed.

Sometimes, a player does not time his or her swing effectively and the transfer of energy is not efficient. Stored elastic energy in muscles disappears quickly once the muscles rebound to their original form. Therefore, if a player is too early or late in their swing, the elastic energy will not transfer efficiently to the ball. Peter Sallay, an orthopedic surgeon who treats tennis athletes, explains,

> Even a millisecond hesitation between the movements of the linked segments in a chain can result in a dramatic decrease in energy transfer. An everyday example is the bull whip. If you raise the whip and in a fluid

Active Versus Stored Energy

The concept of energy helps describe how objects behave the way they do. All objects have kinetic energy and potential energy. If an object is moving, it has kinetic energy. If force is applied to that object, its kinetic energy changes.

Potential energy is stored in an object. For an example, a ball on the ground has potential energy stored in it. To pick up the ball, a person applies a force and lifts it. This work adds energy to the ball and is stored in the ball as potential energy. That is why a ball held 2 feet (0.6m) in the air has more potential energy than a ball held 1 inch (2.5cm) off the ground. When released, the higher ball will hit the ground with more force than the lower ball.

motion snap your arm downwards the end of the whip will crack. If you do the same motion but hesitate for a split second the energy is gone and the whip will behave like a limp noodle.[12]

If a player tries to hit the ball as hard as he or she can, without using proper biomechanics or form, they will not effectively transfer energy to the ball. According to Sallay, recreational tennis players often make this mistake when hitting the ball. A typical mistake occurs when a player uses minimal torso or hip rotation and relies on the shoulder, elbow, and arm to generate speed and power for a shot. Sallay explains,

In this example there is inefficient use of biomechanics. The linkages are disjointed and are less likely to produce the desired effect. Racquet head speed, thus ball velocity will be negatively impacted. Furthermore, this sequence leads to potential injury. There is hardly any use of the elastic energy from trunk and hip rotation and knee bend so the player is "arming the ball" [swinging the ball independently of the rest of the body] which can lead to muscle strain injury.[13]

The Science of the Serve

The tennis serve is one of the most important shots a player makes. Once a player masters the serve, he can use it to his advantage in a match. Professional players, such as Serena Williams and Andy Roddick, use their serve as an offensive weapon. They hit killer serves to gain advantage over an opponent and win points. The ability to return a hard-hit serve is also a critical part of winning a match.

Not only are serves important, but they are also some of the most complicated shots in tennis. During a serve, the player's body twists and rotates and the muscles stretch and contract. These steps transfer energy from the body to the ball, culminating in a ball that rockets at incredible speeds over the net. Roddick has the world's fastest tennis serve. It was once clocked at 155 miles per hour (249kph). To get that speed, Roddick uses more than his arm to power the ball. He has learned how to transfer energy efficiently through the kinetic chain from his large muscle groups in the legs,

SERVING THE BALL

When a player serves the ball the elastic energy transfers from body segment to body segment, from the legs, through the body, to the arm and, eventually, the racket and ball.

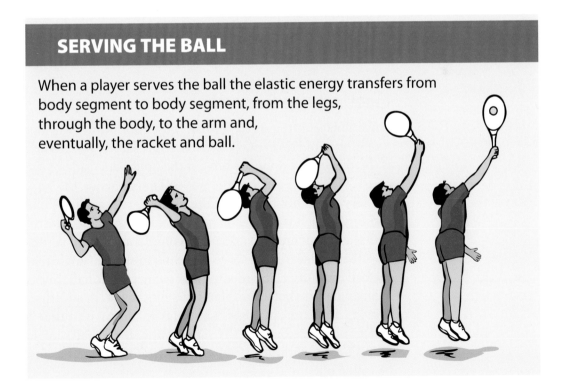

abdomen, and torso. "(Roddick is) using so much legs and so much (body), and that's where he gets his power,"[14] says Brad Gilbert, Roddick's former coach and an ESPN analyst.

To begin a serve, a player tosses the ball into the air. He or she then moves the racket into a windup. Most players start with the racket in front of them and then they swing it down toward the ground, then up behind the shoulder and over the head, and then back down again. At the point the racket strikes the ball, it is pointing in the direction that the player wants the ball to travel. As the racket head moves forward and strikes the ball, it also moves across the back of the ball and causes it to spin. During the windup, the player presses his or her feet against the court. Ground-reaction forces build up elastic energy as do the stretching of muscles in the legs, hips, torso, and shoulders.

Through the windup, the elastic energy transfers from segment to segment in the body from the legs up to the arm and, eventually, the racket and ball. "These contributions vary from person to person, but the data shows the clear importance of the trunk, shoulder internal rotation and wrist flexion in the swing to impact,"[15] says Bruce Elliott, a professor at the University of Western Australia who has studied the physics of tennis.

Getting the Serve In

Once a player hits a serve, the ball must clear the net without touching it and drop into the cross-court service box, which is the diagonally opposite box on the opponent's side of the court. If the ball touches the net or lands outside the box, the serve does not count and the player serves again. While serving the ball with speed and power is important, control and placement are also critical to completing a good serve.

When a player hits a serve, there is a minimum angle that the ball must travel in order to clear the net. If the ball travels at an angle less than this, then it will hit the net. In addition, there is a maximum angle that the ball can have so that it will not bounce beyond the service line. If the ball's angle exceeds the maximum, it will travel beyond the baseline and be called out.

THE TENNIS COURT

On the serve, the tennis ball must clear the net without touching it and drop into the diagonally opposite box on the opponent's side of the court. If the ball hits the net or lands outside the box, the serve is not good.

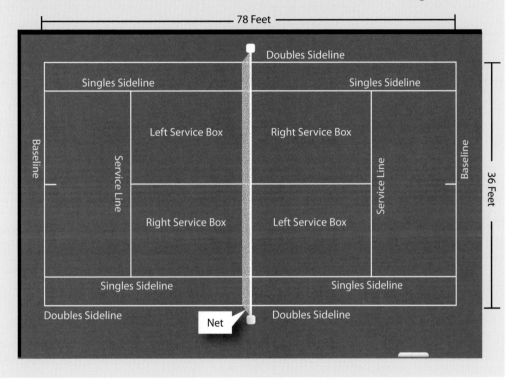

├─────────── 78 Feet ───────────┤

Doubles Sideline

Singles Sideline | Singles Sideline

Left Service Box | Right Service Box

Baseline | Service Line | Service Line | Baseline | 36 Feet

Right Service Box | Left Service Box

Singles Sideline | Singles Sideline

Doubles Sideline | Doubles Sideline

Net

Adapted from www.tennistips.org/how-to-play-tennis.html and www.sporting-central.com/tennis-rules.html.

This minimum-maximum angle range is called the window of acceptance. A player must hit the ball through the window of acceptance in order for a serve to be good. If the window is large, then the ball is more likely to go in. If it is small, then the player is more likely to serve the ball outside the service line and it will be called a foul. The size of the window depends on several factors, including the speed of the ball, the height at which the ball is hit, the ball's spin, and the server's location on the court.

As the ball travels faster, the window of acceptance shrinks. That is why it takes incredible precision to deliver a 120-mile-per-hour (193kph) serve successfully. A slower ball has a larger window of acceptance, because the force of gravity can more easily act upon it, pulling it down into the service box, which is the box on the other side of the net into which the server has to hit the ball.

While many players toss the ball into the air during a serve, the height they toss the ball varies from player to player. When they hit the ball during the toss also varies. Some throw the ball high, while others toss it low. Some players hit the ball almost as soon as they release it, while others will wait a second or two as it falls. Physics plays a role in how the ball will react to the different types of tosses and strikes.

Serves that hit balls high off the ground have a larger acceptance window. Many players reach overhand, jump, and extend their body when hitting a serve. This helps them hit the ball at a higher point, increasing the acceptance window. Impact height is also a reason why taller players have an advantage over shorter players. They can use their height to hit a serve at a higher point, which will give the taller player a better chance of getting the ball in the service box. This is also why many players jump as they hit a serve, enabling them to strike the ball at the highest possible distance from the ground.

In addition, a ball served with topspin also has a larger range of good serve angles. Topspin on the serve creates an area of low pressure underneath the ball, which makes it dive down into the service court. One way players increase topspin on serves is to toss the ball higher during their windup. Balls tossed higher have more time to accelerate as they fall. The faster the ball is falling when it is hit, the more spin it will have. Therefore, the higher the toss, the faster the ball falls and the more spin it will have.

CHAPTER **6**

The Psychology of Tennis

At the highest levels of tennis, many players have the physical strength and skills to succeed. So what separates the winners from the losers? The winners possess the ability to execute physical shots under the pressure of competition. To succeed, players must bring focus and self-confidence to the tennis court. They must be able to recover from mistakes and never let an opponent sense a weakness. In a sea of competition, strong mental skills can set a player apart from his or her opponent. Mental skills are often the difference that determines which players win critical matches and which players fall apart under pressure.

Serbian professional tennis player Novak Djokovic says that mental toughness has helped him win tough matches, including a victory in the 2011 Italian Open over tennis star Rafael Nadal. "Matches between the top players are always very close, and, you know, obviously everybody's hitting the ball well. Everybody is physically fit and practicing hours and hours every day. But, if you have the mental ability to stay strong, stay patient and confident and just have belief in the right moments, then you get a win, you know. So that's what makes the difference,"[16] says Djokovic.

A Mental Game

In tennis players with size, skill, strength, agility, and speed have an edge over their opponents. Yet the game of tennis is just as much about mental ability as it is about physical ability. Even if a player is physically strong, he or she may lose against an opponent who is mentally stronger. This explains why a forty-year-old recreational player can beat a twenty-year-old who hits harder shots and runs faster

Champion player Kim Clijsters has commented that the mental aspect of tennis is as important a factor in a player's success as the physical game.

across the court. The forty-year-old is likely more disciplined, calm, and focused during the match, using his mental skills to his advantage.

Mental skills help athletes control their minds as they compete or perform, allowing them to adjust their actions, reactions, thoughts, and feelings and use them to improve their performance. Mental skills may help a player improve self-confidence, focus, and concentration; deal with stress and adversity; and react positively to errors.

Players who have strong mental skills and a strong mental tennis game will have an advantage over their opponents. John H. Sklare, a USPTA (United States Professional Tennis Association) certified tennis professional and doctor of educational psychology, explains,

> In a nutshell, success on the tennis court takes more than just physical prowess and weekly stroke production. I know far too many people who hit like a pro during practice and warm up but, once the match starts, a whole new mindset emerges and an entirely different team seems to take the field. Why is it that so many of you can't find an inkling of your game once the match starts? In my opinion, it's because tennis is much more than a mere physical sport. It is also very much a mental game as well. It is those who practice and hone both mental and physical skills that find themselves on the winning side most often.[17]

The top tennis players sharpen their mental skills and use their experiences to help them anticipate, prepare for, and meet challenges. Kim Clijsters, a Belgian professional tennis player who retired in 2012, says that challenging matches that tested her mental and physical strength and stamina occurred regularly. "So the stress will always be there. It's a part of the sport, and the mental game is just so important, as well,"[18] she says.

Emotions on the Court

Tennis is a highly emotional game. It pits one player against another in a tense personal battle. Each match is a battle of wills where only one winner will emerge. Justin Gimelstob,

Roadmap to Victory: The Game Plan

Before the start of a game, top tennis players plan how they will approach the match. They study their opponents and learn their strengths and weaknesses. They also evaluate their own strengths and weaknesses. Then they use that information to develop a winning game plan.

A game plan is a road map for a player to use in a match that maximizes his or her strengths and minimizes weaknesses. At the same time, the game plan should take advantage of opponents' weaknesses and limit their opportunities to use their strengths. For example, if an opponent tends to be aggressive at the baseline, then a player should hit more short balls to force the opponent into errors. If an opponent has a great forehand shot but a weaker backhand, then a good game plan concentrates on sending balls that force the opponent to use his backhand.

a broadcaster and a retired American professional tennis player, says,

> I contend that tennis is the toughest sport in the world. It is emotional by its very nature, and it's the only sport that demands so many different types of physical and mental skill sets. And it all takes place while you stand alone in a gladiatorial ring thinly disguised as a simple tennis court. But there is nothing simple or serene about it. Competitive tennis is a battle![19]

In highly competitive matches, players may find it difficult to control their emotions. The constant ups and downs of tennis can take a toll on players, leaving them drained. Win a dramatic point and a player becomes elated. Double-fault—hitting the net, stepping over the baseline, or hitting outside the service box—on a serve and elation turns to despair. When a match is close, a player may get tense. This can lead to breakdowns in technique or to rushing his or her

Fernando Gonzalez smashes his racquet onto the court in frustration during a tournament in 2006. Tennis players sometimes react to mistakes, bad calls, or bad luck on the court with strong emotions.

shots, either of which may result in mistakes on the court. Many players react emotionally when they make a mistake. They get mad. Some throw tantrums, curse, and hit their racket against the closest object.

Not only can emotions disrupt a player's game, but they can also cause them to lose a match. In 2012 David Nalbandian, an Argentine professional tennis player, was disqualified from the AEGON Championships and fined more than twelve thousand dollars for a tantrum on the court. During the match, Nalbandian smashed an advertising panel after losing his serve, cutting the line judge's leg and causing it to bleed heavily. "Sometimes you get angry, sometimes you cannot control when that happens," said Nalbandian, who later apologized. "I am very sorry, sometimes you get frustrated on court,"[20] he said. Nalbandian also had to forfeit more than fifty-seven thousand dollars in prize money from the tournament.

Keeping a Positive Mindset

Instead of letting negative emotions overcome them, successful players learn that thinking positively is key to winning in tennis. Every player makes mistakes during a match. They may choose the wrong shot to hit. They may execute a serve poorly or miss an easy forehand shot. Yet it is how they recover from mistakes that determine their overall performance and the ultimate outcome of the match.

Tennis psychologists suggest several ways players can stay positive even when a match is not going well. Some examples include positive self-talk before a game point, staying enthusiastic during the match, and pumping up with positive thoughts after winning a big point. Managing emotions can be difficult, especially when losing, but it is important to help the player maintain clear judgement and stay motivated.

Dealing with Pressure

Playing professional tennis can be very stressful. Sometimes, the stress in tennis is physical. Matches can extend for hours at a time, sometimes being delayed because of rain or other unforeseen reasons. The longest Wimbledon match lasted four hours and forty-eight minutes in 2008 between Rafael Nadal and Roger Federer. Noise, weather, and bad calls from the officials can add even more stress during a match.

Other times stress is mental and is called pressure. Tennis players experience pressure in many ways. Fearing failure, they put pressure on themselves to win. They may also feel pressure from the expectations of coaches, family, and fans. If the match is important, then players may feel heightened pressure to perform well. This pressure may be magnified by other factors. Playing against a feared opponent or in front of a heckling crowd, for example, can cause a player's stress and pressure levels to skyrocket.

A tearful Jan Novotna is consoled by the Duchess of Kent after losing to Steffi Graff in the 1993 Wimbledon finals.

Pressure is inherent to tennis. How players react to it can make or break their game. Some players seem to rise to the occasion and play their best under pressure. American Pete Sampras, one of the greatest tennis players in the history of the game, won fourteen Grand Slam titles during his career from 1988 to 2003. He was a calm player on the court, holding in his emotions and working through every point, game, and match. One of Sampras's greatest assets was his ability to perform well under pressure, no matter the match or the opponent.

Some situations are more stressful than others. In the final set of the Wimbledon finals, every point feels impossibly important. Millions of people around the world are watching the match, and its outcome may depend on whether or not a player can make one great serve. Whether a tennis player succeeds or "chokes" in this situation depends on how he or she deals with pressure.

Pressure can be helpful and harmful to players. Some pressure can be good, when it stimulates adrenaline and allows players to play to their highest abilities. In some situations, though, high pressure can negatively affect an athlete. When it causes athletes to doubt their abilities, the pressure may lead them to overthink their performance. They can become overly conscious of their movements, analyzing each forehand, backhand, and serve. This intense focus can affect players' mechanics and adversely affect their performance. It stiffens their muscles and makes the simplest shots difficult. Breathing becomes rapid and judgment is impaired. Some players under stress develop cramps or back spasms or they simply lose their natural flow and rhythm in a game.

One of the most famous examples of choking in tennis occurred in the 1993 Wimbledon final. Jana Novotná of the Czech Republic led Steffi Graf of Germany in the sixth game of the deciding set of the finals. By winning her next service point, Novotná could take a 5–1 lead over Graff. Yet Novotná double-faulted on the serve. The pressure became too much and she fell apart. She continued to miss serves and misplay easy volleys. About ten minutes later, Graf had won Wimbledon, coming back to win the final set 6–4.

Rituals

To help themselves remain calm and mentally focused on the court, tennis players often develop rituals that help them feel in control. Rituals, the habits a player repeats before or during a game, may help them to regroup and refocus or to calm their nerves. Belarusian professional tennis player Victoria Azarenka has a prematch routine of warming up to music. She enters each arena with her headphones on and hoodie up. Maria Sharapova has a slow, deliberate routine before each serve that includes taking balls from the same corner of the court, walking to the baseline and bouncing the ball, tucking her hair behind her ears, and bouncing the ball twice

before finally serving. "We all have our own routines. Some players take more time. Some not so much. So, you know, it's just important to focus on your own thing and what's your ritual before returning or serving,"[21] says top-ranked Ana Ivanović, a Serbian professional tennis player.

Maria Sharapova tucks her hair behind her ear as part of her pre-serve ritual during a U.S. Open match in 2007.

Sports psychology tends to support these rituals as having a positive impact on player performance. Psychologists say that if a ritual improves a player's confidence, it can be a factor in a player performing better and succeeding. In addition, rituals that involve athletic routines, such as bouncing a ball before a serve, can boost an athlete's performance by focusing his or her attention and preparing the body's motor sequences. "An athlete's routine is critical. The body is a marvelous piece of machinery, but you can interfere with it. If you see the basketball player at the free throw line, you will often notice a certain routine being repeated. That is when negative thoughts are being replaced by positive thoughts, relaxation occurs and mistakes are minimized,"[22] says Richard Cox, a sports psychology researcher at the University of Missouri-Columbia.

Focus and Concentration

To play their best, world-class players maintain intense focus during a match. Focus is the ability to pay attention to things that are important and ignore those that are not. Some of the best tennis players are known for their ability to focus on the things that matter and that they can control during a match.

Focusing in tennis is not an easy task, because there is a lot of competition for a player's attention. The crowd, the weather, even the opponent can distract a player from concentrating on the game. During a match, these types of distractions can draw a player's attention away from his next shot or his opponent's serve. At the beginning of a match, many players find it easy to concentrate, but as the hours wear on, a player's focus may diminish. Little distractions like a fan coughing in the stands or an opponent's shoes squeaking may distract a player and take some of his or her focus away from the game.

Dominating the Opponent

A tennis match is a struggle between two people, a test of will and mental strength. Tennis champions use mental skills to dominate their opponents, adding one more weapon to

Rafael Nadal pumps his fist and shouts after a good shot during a U.S. Open finals match in 2010. Nadal's on-court behavior and body language have been known to intimidate some opponents.

their arsenal. According to Allen Fox, a former tennis player and coach, players dominate the court when they make lesser players feel inferior, which makes them play worse. For example, Roger Federer, with his imposing physical presence, has often intimidated his opponents simply by standing across the net from them. They felt defeated before they even started the match. As a result, they missed shots that they easily made against other opponents. Federer's opponents are more likely than normal to become nervous or get discouraged when they fall behind during a match. Much of Federer's dominance comes from the way he carries himself on the court, confident and unaffected by his opponent's wins.

Dominant players show no weakness to their opponent. They keep their heads up, stride steady, and their game under control no matter what the situation. Rafael Nadal uses body language on the court to intimidate opponents. He walks

Sports Psychologist

Psychologists are health professionals who specialize in the diagnosis and treatment of mental and emotional disorders. They study mental processes and human behavior. They observe how people relate to one another and the environment. Psychologists work in schools, hospitals, clinics, and for large companies. They are not medical doctors, but they do have a master's, specialist, or doctoral degree in psychology. Most states require that practicing psychologists have a license or certification.

Sports psychologists specialize in working with athletes of all levels. They may work with teams or individual athletes. Sport psychologists help athletes overcome problems, enhance performance, and achieve goals. Among the mental skills they can teach athletes are the use of visualization to enhance performance and various strategies to deal with pressure from coaches, family, and their own expectations. Sports psychologists may show an athlete ways to overcome anxiety or loss of focus during competition. They may also work with injured athletes using techniques such as guided imagery to visualize healing.

Sports psychology is a growing profession. Many athletes hire psychologists to help them with the mental side of sports training and competition. Research shows that at elite levels of sport mental training skills, such as focus, relaxation, and reducing anxiety, can be critical factors between first and second place. Motivation, concentration, and focus are also helpful skills for recreational athletes.

quickly between points. He keeps his head and shoulders up, never slumped, at all times, rarely showing frustration, and he celebrates his good shots with a fist pump. "Sometimes this is the reason why accomplished athletes are considered cocky," said Cox. "They need to be; they cannot be thinking negative thoughts."[23]

Self-Confidence

The root of every player's mental skills is self-confidence. Players that have self-confidence usually have an edge over their opponents. They believe they can win, and with this belief supporting them, they approach a match with excitement rather than fear. This makes them better able to play at their highest level, rather than becoming tight and making mental mistakes. A player without confidence is more likely to be shaky and perform poorly. Federer showed his mental toughness and confidence in his 2012 Wimbledon victory over Englishman Andy Murray. Throughout the match, Federer believed in his strategy and ability to win. "This is, I guess, how you want to win Wimbledon—by going after your shots, believing you can do it," Federer said after the match, "and that's what I was able to do today."[24]

Many players have strategies to improve their confidence. Some meditate about winning, repeating a mantra such as, "I am going to win." Others visualize hitting winning shots and lifting the championship trophy. Others use positive self-talk, reminding themselves of their powerful serve or efficient backhands. Sampras pumped himself up before a match. In his book, *A Champion's Mind: Lessons from a Life in Tennis*, Sampras writes,

> It might strike some as arrogant, but that's the kind of fuel you need to really reach the heights of achievement. There were times in my career where I would step up to the service line at a crucial moment in the heat of the moment in a big match and pause to drink in the atmosphere. Fired up by adrenaline, I'd look toward the crowd and defiantly say to myself, *All right, everybody, now I'm going to show you who I really am.*[25]

Davis Cup captain John McEnroe, left, consoles Vince Spadea after his loss in a semifinal match in 2000, a year during which Spadea's self-confidence tumbled along with his level of play.

A player's confidence can move in cycles, through slumps and streaks. The more a player wins, the more his confidence increases. Eventually, however, all players experience some losses, which can cause their confidence to waver. This can lead to further losses and a decline of confidence. The downward spiral continues until the player finds a way to win and his confidence begins to rebound.

American Vince Spadea's professional tennis career is an example of how confidence can affect a player. In 1999 Spadea reached an Association of Tennis Professionals (ATP) world ranking at number 19. His confidence in his ability on the court was also at an all-time high. The following year,

Spadea suffered a record twenty-one straight first-round tournament losses. With each loss, his confidence fell further, making it harder for him to win his next match. His ranking plummeted to number 233 and his confidence in his abilities fell to an all-time low. Eventually Spadea rebounded. By playing in a few minor tournaments to get some wins, he built up his confidence. He eventually rose to a ranking of number 18 in 2005.

Players use several tactics to build and rebuild their confidence. Some will set up matches with weaker opponents in order to get some wins and boost their confidence. Others change coaches to give them a fresh voice or new approach. In 1994 when Andre Agassi, an American professional tennis player, was faltering, he called upon Coach Brad Gilbert for help. Gilbert gave Agassi new technical information but also provided him with new hope and motivation. Gilbert helped boost Agassi's confidence, and he won six majors while Gilbert was his coach.

As Spadea's experience demonstrates, mistakes can have a negative effect on confidence. Players who think their mistakes are failures have lower self-confidence. Other players learn to view mistakes as an important part of learning and improving their game. Players who can learn from their mistakes, shake them off, and move on to the next point or match have a better chance of succeeding than those who wallow in a mistake, unable to forget about it.

Today's tennis tour is full of players with wicked serves, killer forehands, and amazing stamina. While some matches are won with physical skills, many more are decided by less obvious mental skills. The most powerful weapon in the player's bag is his or her mental toughness. When both opponents are on equal footing physically, the player who can focus better, calmly accept mistakes, and believe in his or her ability to win will most likely be the player who takes home the trophy. Sklare explains,

It's errors not winners that ultimately determine who wins most matches. If you want to work smarter not harder on the tennis court and improve both your enjoyment and your winning percentage, take heed of the following: identify your opponents weakness[es]

and hammer them relentlessly; learn how to effectively handle pressure and stay calm at all times; focus on the point at hand and block out distractions; avoid getting psyched-out or intimidated by bad calls and gamesmanship; quickly bounce back after an error and then get mentally prepared for the next point; eliminate negative thinking and start to think like a winner. What an incredible difference these ingredients can make in your game! That, my dear friend, is the recipe for working more mental muscle into this wonderful game!"[26]

NOTES

Chapter 1: The History of Tennis

1. Quoted in "Tennis: I Love It Too Much to Quit, Says Serena." *New Zealand Herald*, June 25, 2012. www.nzherald.co.nz/tennis/news/article.cfm?c_id=94&objectid=10815242.

2. Quoted in Chris Lehourites. "Top 10 from 10 Different Countries in WTA Rankings." *Washington Times*, January 31, 2011. www.washingtontimes.com/news/2011/jan/31/top-10-from-10-different-countries-in-wta-rankings/?page=all.

3. Quoted in Brian Bouchard. "Spencer William Gore (1850–1906)." Epsom and Ewell History Explorer. www.epsomandewellhistoryexplorer.org.uk/Gore.html.

4. Quoted in Geoff MacDonald. "How the Serve Went Over the Top." *New York Times*, August 28, 2011. www.nytimes.com/2011/08/29/sports/tennis/the-genteel-origins-of-tennis-and-the-serve.html?pagewanted=all.

5. Quoted in "Robert Kelleher, Open Era Pioneer in U.S., Dies."
Grips, June 21, 2012. http://www.gripsprogram.com/node/3304.

6. Quoted in Melinda Samson. "Interview with Former ATP Slam Champion and Current Tennis Australia Manager Scott Draper." Tennis Grandstand, May 25, 2012. http://www.tennisgrandstand.com/2012/05/25/interview-with-former-atp-slam-champion-and-current-tennis-australia-manager-scott-draper/.

7. Chris McKendry. "I Also Play Tennis." *Tennis View Magazine*, June 14, 2012.

Chapter 2: Training and Conditioning

8. Paul Roetert and Todd Ellenbecker. *Complete Conditioning for Tennis*. Champaign, IL: Human Kinetics, 2007. p. 3.

9. Quoted in Ed McGrogan. "Plyometric Training with Elena Dementieva." Tennis.com, September 25, 2009. www.tennis.com/articles/templates/fitness.aspx?articleid=1146&zoneid=19.

Chapter 3: Racket Power and Control

10. Rod Cross and Crawford Lindsey. *Technical Tennis: Racquets, Strings, Balls, Courts, Spin, and Bounce.* Vista, CA: Racquet Tech, 2005. p. 9.
11. Quoted in Ed McGrogan. "Spin Ball: The Physics of Polyester String." Tennis.com, February 3, 2011. http://tennis.com/articles/templates/gear.aspx?articleid=10312&zoneid=24.

Chapter 5: Getting the Ball in the Box

12. Peter Sallay. "Biomechanics of Tennis." USTA Midwest, January 16, 2007. www.midwest.usta.com/News/2007_01/395352_Biomechanics_of_Tennis.
13. Sallay. "Biomechanics of Tennis."
14. Quoted in "Tennis' Sonic Boom." *USA Today*, www.usatoday.com/sports/tennis/andy-roddick-serve.htm.
15. Quoted in Tom Colligan. "Tennis Physics: Anatomy of a Serve." *Popular Mechanics*, December 18, 2009. www.popularmechanics.com/outdoors/sports/physics/4221210#ixzz1pJIjbA2i.

Chapter 6: The Psychology of Tennis

16. Quoted in Patrick Cohn. "Djokovic's Mental Game: Riding the Momentum." Sports Psychology for Tennis, May 20, 2011. www.sportspsychologytennis.com/?p=3496.
17. John H. Sklare. "Play Smarter Not Harder." USTA Atlanta. www.atlanta.usta.com/Atlanta_Tennis/Play_Smarter_Not_Harderby_Dr_John_H_Sklare/.
18. Quoted in Patrick Cohn. "Kim Clijsters Beats Wozniaki with a Strong Mental Game." Sports Psychology for Tennis, January 25, 2012. www.sportspsychologytennis.com/?p=3646.
19. Quoted in Allen Fox. *Tennis: Winning the Mental Match.* Kearney, NE: Morris, 2010. p. v.
20. Quoted in "David Nalbandian Explains Criticism After Disqualification." BBC, June 17, 2012. www.bbc.co.uk/sport/0/tennis/18480270.
21. Ana Ivanovi . Interview: Australian Open. ASAP Sports, January 24, 2008. www.asapsports.com/show_interview.php?id=47257.

22. Quoted in "Athlete's 'Rituals' Important for Overcoming Performance Anxiety." PHYS.org, January 31, 2007. http://phys.org/news89468913.html#jCp.
23. Quoted in "Athlete's 'Rituals' Important for Overcoming Performance Anxiety."
24. Quoted in Exact Sports Blog. "Roger Federer: Calm Under Pressure." Blog entry by Trevor, July 10, 2012. http://exactsports.com/blog/roger-federer-calm-under-pressure/2012/07/10/.
25. Pete Sampras. *A Champion's Mind: Lessons from a Life in Tennis*. With Peter Bodo. New York: Crown, 2008. p. xi.
26. Sklare. "Play Smarter Not Harder."

GLOSSARY

aerobic: Occurring only in the presence of oxygen.

anaerobic: Occurring in the absence of oxygen.

concentric action: The phase of plyometric exercise during which the muscle contracts and applies its force.

dynamic stretching: A method of stretching muscles that includes moving them through the joint's range of motion.

eccentric action: A movement in which muscle fibers lengthen and stretch.

force: Any outside stress that causes an object to move or change its shape.

friction: The resistance put on a moving object by another surface that causes it to slow down.

kinetic energy: The form of energy involved in movement.

Magnus effect: The force on a spinning object that causes it to change its path in flight.

mass: The amount of matter contained in an object.

plyometrics: A method of power training that puts the muscles in a prestretch before executing a powerful contraction.

static stretching: Stretching a muscle with a slow movement that is held in place for twenty to thirty seconds.

FOR MORE INFORMATION

Books

Patricia Bow. *Tennis Science*. New York: Crabtree, 2009.
Good overview of science related to tennis.

Anne K. Brown. *People in the News*: *Roger Federer*. Farmington Hills, MI: Lucent Books, 2012. Biography about the life and career of tennis great Roger Federer.

Jacqueline Edmondson. *Venus and Serena Williams: A Biography*. Westport, CT: Greenwood, 2005. Biography of tennis stars Venus and Serena Williams.

Paul Roetert and Todd Ellenbecker. *Complete Conditioning for Tennis*. Champaign, IL: Human Kinetics, 2007. Details exercises, drills, and programs designed to improve tennis performance.

Venus Williams and Serena Williams. *Venus & Serena: Serving from the Hip; 10 Rules for Living, Loving, and Winning*, with Hilary Beard. Boston: Mifflin, 2005. Tennis stars Venus and Serena Williams offer advice to teens.

Websites

International Tennis Federation (www.itftennis.com). This is the website of the world governing body of tennis. It includes brief articles about balls, rackets, strings, and courts and how they affect the game of tennis.

International Tennis Hall of Fame & Museum (www.tennisfame.com). This site offers brief biographies on hall of fame players and a history of tennis in the United States.

United States Tennis Association (www.usta.com). This site offers information about strength training, biomechanics, sports medicine, and other topics related to the science of tennis.

INDEX

A

ABC *Wide World of Sports*, 6
Acceleration, 7, 29
Acute injuries, 25
Adenosine triphosphate (ATP), 38, 39
AEGON Championships, 83
Aerobic activities, 37–39
Aerodynamics, 6
African Americans, 9, *9*
Agassi, Andre, 93
Agility, 24, *28*, 28–29
Agility drills, *28*, 29
Airflow, 71
Allaster, Stacey, 10
All England Croquet Club, 14, 15
Aluminum frame, 42
Amateur tennis, 22
American Tennis Association (ATA), 9
    National Championships of, 9
Anaerobic activities, 37–39
Angle of incidence, 62
Angle of reflection, *61*, 62
Arm circles, 27
Arming the ball, 74
Ashe, Arthur, 9, *9*
Ashe, Arthur, Stadium, 9
Ash wood, 42
Association of Tennis Professionals
    (ATP), 22, 92
    tournaments of, 57
    tour of, 22

Australian Open, 9, 18, 20
Azarenka, Victoria, 86

B

Backhand shot, *30*, 31, 33, 71
Back pain, 25
Backspin, 69, 71
Balance point, 46
Baseline players, 65
Bicep curl, 35
Biceps, 33, 35
Biomechanics, 6, 74
Bogataj, Vinko, 6
Bones, 29
The Book of the Game (Wingfield), 13
Borotra, Jean, 19
Brugnon, Jacques, 19
Budge, Don, 9

C

Career Grand Slam, 20
Cartilage, torn, 25
Center of gravity, 6
Center of percussion (COP), *48*, 49–50
*A Champion's Mind: Lessons from a
    Life in Tennis* (Sampras), 91
Cheating, 7
Clijsters, Kim, *80*, 81
Cochet, Henri, 19
Coefficient of friction (COF), 64

PICTURE CREDITS

Cover images: © Sashkin/Shutterstock.com, © hkeita/Shutterstock.com, © bikerideriondon/Shutterstock.com

© AP Images/Cesar Rangel, 92

© AP Images/Denis Paquin, 85

© AP Images/Mark Baker, 83

© AP Images/Mark Humphrey, 28

© AP Images/Mark J. Terrill, 38

© Chris McGrath/Getty Images, 89

© Chris Trotman/Getty Images for USTA, 69

© cjmac/Shutterstock.com, 34

© Clive Brunskill/Getty Images, 80

© dk/Alamy, 56

© dotshock/Shutterstock.com, 43

© Emmanuel Dunand/AFP/Getty Images, 87

© ER_09/Shutterstock.com, 42

© Focus on Sport/Getty Images, 9

© Gale, Cengage Learning, 32, 36, 48, 61, 75, 77

© Getty Images, 17

© Hulton Archive/Getty Images, 19

© Imagestate Media Partners Limit - Impact Photos/Alamy, 59

© INTERFOTO/Alamy, 12

© Jasper Juinen/Getty Images, 30

© jstudio/Shutterstock.com, 25

© Maxisport/Shutterstock.com, 44

© Michael Cole/Alamy, 67

© North Wind Picture Archives/The Image Works, 15

© Olga Besnard/Shutterstock.com, 63

© PCN Photography/Alamy, 52

© Rob Dack/Shutterstock.com, 72

© Supri Suharjoto/Shutterstock.com, 27

© Ted Kinsman/Science Source/Photo Researchers, Inc., 51

© Terry Oakley/Alamy, 58

© Universal History Archive/Getty Images, 14

© Universal/TempSport/Corbis, 21

ABOUT THE AUTHOR

Carla Mooney is the author of several books for young readers. She loves investigating new ideas and learning about how the world works. A graduate of the University of Pennsylvania, Mooney lives in Pittsburgh with her husband and three children.